From My Mother's
House of Beauty
by Susan Stephanie Henry

Neighborhood Story Project

P.O. Box 19742

New Orleans, LA 70179

www.neighborhoodstoryproject.org

Editor: Rachel Breunlin

Publisher: Abram Himelstein

Graphic Designer: Gareth Breunlin

The printing of this book made possible by
a generous grant from the Lupin Foundation.

THE
LUPIN
FOUNDATION

ISBN-13: 978-1-60801-014-1

Library of Congress Control Number: 2009940211

http://unopress.uno.edu

Dedication

I dedicate this book to my mom. You make me feel proud of who I am. Because you passed your talents on to me. Because you inspire me to be the best that I can be. Because you did a lot of things I know you didn't mean. Because you could light up a room with your way of being. For being my girlfriend. For giving me your name. I hated it at first, but I'm you, in my own special way.

Acknowledgements

Thank you:

To my parents for being my inspiration to be successful: My mother for being the best mother in the world and my daddy for sharing your stories.

To my grandparents for pushing me to be all I can be, and teaching me about my history.

To Mrs. Rich for being such a pain in my butt and punching my arm when I would get a wrong answer on those 100 question tests. For pushing me to be all I can be.

To my boss Janice for making one of my dreams a reality.

To the Fashion Institute of New Orleans for acknowledging my hard work and dedication, and for helping with pictures.

To Uncle Henry for always giving me help and support.

To Uncle Cregg for always putting a smile on my face.

To my grams back home for always giving me strength.

To my little brother for being my friend. I hope you don't try to get me back for all the times I was mean to you. For keeping my secrets even when I told yours. Sorry. For taking the key for us to drive around in Dad's car. That's how I learned to drive. For eating all the stuff I cook and saying you like it.

I want to thank Uncle David for all of the wonderful trips.

To Nikky for being my first best friend. I love you, cousin.

To DeeDee for being my friend first and then my cousin.

To Abram for helping me not sound cliché.

To Rachel for being an awesome editor. You helped bring my stories to life.

To Kenneth, Kareem, and Daron for giving good feedback on my stories and for making me laugh when writing seemed hard.

To Pernell for keeping it real.

To Lea for being a good listener and a great help for my pieces.

To Lindsey for helping with my interviews.

To Felipe and Carolina for sharing your family stories.

To my book committee: Mrs. Richardson, Jainey Bavishi, and my dad and brother. Thank you very much for taking time to read and talk about a draft of my book.

Thank you to Daniel Hammer and the Historic New Orleans Collection, Hortensia Calvo and David Dressing at the Latin American Library at Tulane University, and Irene Wainwright at the City Archives of the New Orleans Public Library for additional maps and images of La Ceiba.

To Hanna for being someone I can admire.

To the pastor at my church for being so great at preaching. You always gives me a great message.

To anyone reading this book. Thank you.

Table of Contents

INTRODUCTION   1

PART I: GROWING UP IN LA CEIBA

Beautiful Woman   4

Interview with My Dad, Alston Henry, Part I   5

La Julia   8

Interview with My Uncle, Earl Henry Brooks, Part I   9

Grams Comes to Visit   14

Beauty Salon   15

A Little Sister   16

Alston Emmanuel   17

They Called It Depression   18

When is This Day Coming?   19

PART II: NEW ORLEANS

The Day I Came to the States   23

Nikky   24

Different   26

Interview with Felipe Smith, Part I   27

ESL Class   39

Interview with My Grams, Elenor Watler   40

Interview with My Grandpa, Andres Watler   46

Bruxelles   48

Interview with My Dad, Part II   49

What's Yo Name?   53

Sewing Machine   54

Evacuation   55

PART III: RETURNS

Back to La Ceiba 58

Passport 59

School in Houston 60

Not Again 61

Too Small 62

Red 63

My First Boyfriend 64

Interview with Uncle Henry, Part II 66

PART III: INDEPENDENT WOMAN

She's Gone 72

Interview with My Dad, Part III 73

Interview with Mrs. Richardson 75

Different Methods 88

Punishments 89

Saved Up for Me 91

Design 94

Black Hair 102

Interview with Carolina Gallop 104

Interview with Felipe Smith, Part II 113

MAP OF THE

CENTRAL AMERICAN

REPUBLICS

Introduction

I was born in La Ceiba, a city on the Caribbean coast of Honduras. I lived in a neighborhood called Englishtown in a two-story house near the ocean. From our front porch, we could see the deep blue water touch the sky. The scent was nice and fresh. At night, we could see the stars.

In 2000, when I was ten years old, my mom, brother, and I moved to start a new life in New Orleans with my dad. It was a dramatic change—different school, different lifestyle. In La Ceiba, I could run down the street barefoot and onto the beach. I felt far away from the sea. I missed the horizon and being able to tell what time it was just by the light.

In this new place, it was hard for me to talk about where I came from. I said Honduras but over the years, my memory became blurry and I wanted to leave my life in La Ceiba behind. Before I started writing this book, I had no interest in learning about my background. I never paid attention to the reason why I spoke English and most people in my neighborhood in Honduras did not.

I asked my grams once about how our ancestors are connected to the Caribbean coast of Honduras. We are a mixture of Spanish, English, French, Indian, and African. But what does this mean? And how do I explain it to people in New Orleans?

Thanks to several interviews with family members and people from the Honduran community in New Orleans, I learned much more about my roots. The book became a way to help me learn about where I come from and explain to people who don't know.

My family talks about going back to la Ceiba. I, on the other hand, feel attached to both the U.S. and Honduras, particularly New Orleans. One of the bridges between my two places in the world is my mother, who moved back to Honduras in 2007.

My mother was my main inspiration growing up. I got my love for hair and fashion from her. At her salon, she did all kinds of women's hair. Color didn't matter, anyone could come to my mom's shop. Although she isn't here now, I kept what she passed on to me and made it my own.

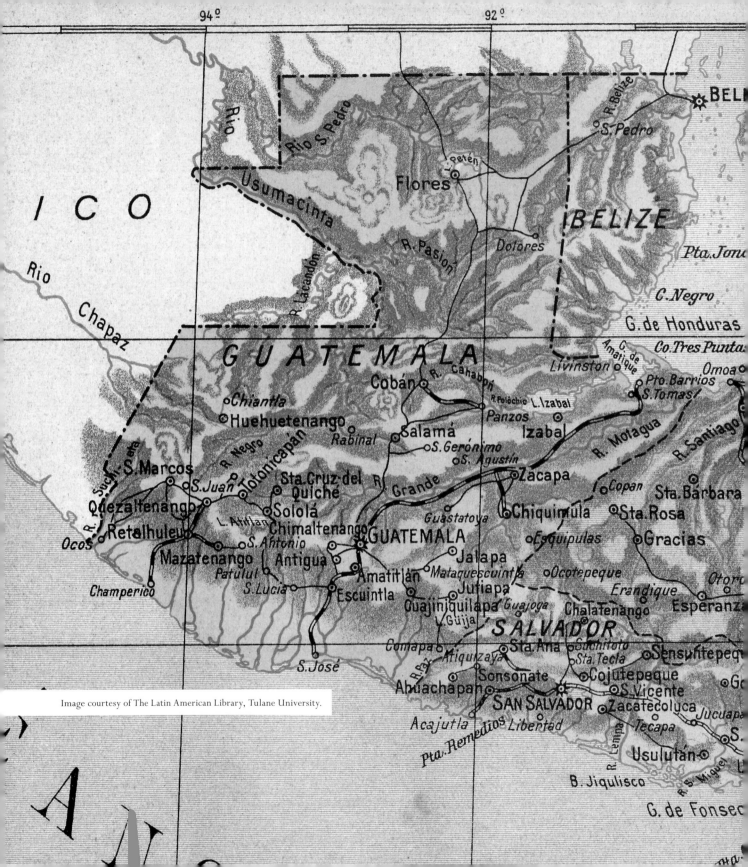

Image courtesy of The Latin American Library, Tulane University.

MAR DE

Turneff

Islas

Coxen Hole
I. Utila
C. Honduras
Cabo Camerón
Trujillo
Iriona
L. Brus
Pta. Patuca
Cortes
La Ceiba
R. Romano
R. Negro
R. Patuco
L. Caratusca
Pedro Sula
R. León
C. Falso
Cabo Gracias á Dios
Yoro
Cabo de Gracias
HONDURAS
S. Cristóbal
Segovia
C. Mosquit
Sulaco
Juticapa
Comayagua
R. Coco ó
Wawa
TEGUCIGALPA
Rio
Yuscorán
R. Prinzapolka
Choluteca
Ocotal
Nacaome
S. Rafael del Norte
Cuicuina
Corpus
Somoto
Esteli
R. Tooma
Choluteca
Jinotega
Negro
Somotillo
R. Estero
Sauce
Matagalpa
R. Grande de Matagalpa
Viejo
Metapa
NICARAGUA
Laguna
de
Cos. Tyra
Chinandega
R. Murra

3

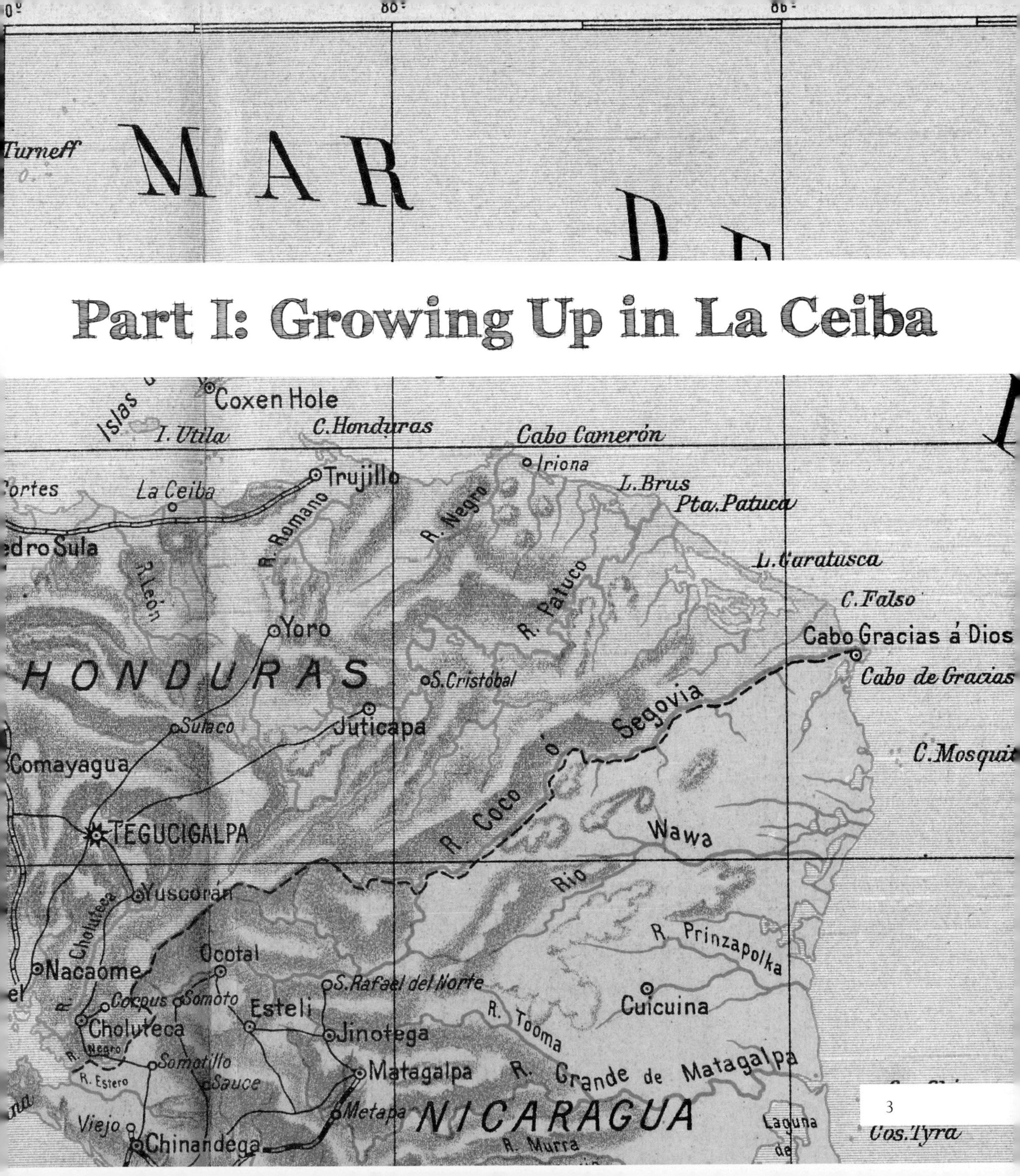

A Beautiful Woman

My name is Susan. It sounds the same and reads the same in both English and Spanish. It was my mother's name. My mom is and always was a beautiful woman. She has dark brown eyes and hair with a small waist.

Everywhere we went, men told her how lucky my dad was. One time, my mom was sitting in front of our house. A man was walking by and saw her sitting there. He started talking to her, trying to get at her, even though he knew she was married. I was so mad, I ran inside, filled a bucket of water and poured it over his head. I didn't feel sorry either.

My dad worked in the States and came home for Christmas time, or a little earlier if he could. He sent boxes of baby clothes and toys. When I was six, I graduated from kindergarten. My mom had a beautiful pink dress handmade for me and gave me my first perm. She bought jewelry for me and dressed me like her because I liked to copy off her.

We took a lot of pictures to send to my dad. I remember one time my mom bought me some shoes like hers. She told me how to pose. I looked like a younger version of her.

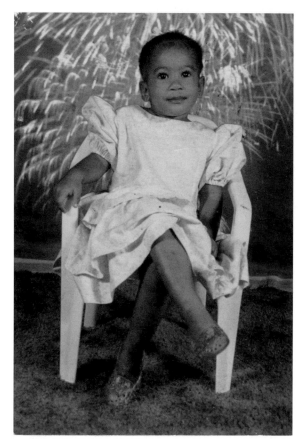

Photograph of Susan sent to her father in the States, courtesy of the Henry family.

Interview with My Dad, Alston Henry, Part I

My dad was staying in the States, but I was still attached to him. We didn't have a phone at home. When he was away, my mom would bring me with her to a teleboutique where we could call out of the country. Sometimes I'd sit on the floor of the booth, and sometimes she'd tell me to give her some privacy and I'd run between the glass boxes, pretending to make my own calls. If he hadn't heard from us in awhile, he'd buy a calling card or sneak and use his mom's phone in New Orleans to call La Ceiba direct. He called the neighbors or my grandmother, and left a message letting us know when he'd call back.

I always wished he would come home—just having him around was nice. Sometimes he'd stay in Honduras for a whole year, but then would have to go back to the U.S. or he'd have problems with his papers.

In La Ceiba, he'd cooked while my mom was working at home, and then would go down the street to his little chill spot in Englishtown. In the backyard, he had a welding shop, and worked on projects for people in the neighborhood. I know he loved being home and the way my mom took care of him, but we didn't talk that much. When my mama cooked, she gave me a plate to give to him. I'd take it into his bedroom where he watching T.V. We didn't eat at the table. Sometimes, my mama laid a sheet down on the floor and I'd bring my plate into his room and watch scary English-speaking movies on Cinemax and HBO with him. We didn't need to read the subtitles because we spoke English.

I don't really conversate with my dad about his past. I wanted to get him to open up and tell some of the stories about how he met my mom, why he moved to the States, and what it was like to live apart from us. I got a lot of stories that I had never heard before. For the first time, I sat with him and heard him speak.

Susan's mother in La Ceiba, courtesy of the Henry family.

Susan: How did you meet Mom?

Alston: That's a long story. I think I was 22 and she was four years younger than me. I saw her walking in Barrio La Julia and I said, "Who the hell is that lady?" My friend told me she stayed in the neighborhood and I said, "Okay, I would like to talk to her." He told me she didn't talk to anybody. She looked like she was very proud. Well, a couple weeks after, I went to my friend and asked him, "What she tell you?" She told him she wanted to meet me. She had liked me for awhile, too.

S: What attracted you to her?

A: You know, she was a beautiful lady—she had a nice looking body, a sexy walk, and everybody wanted to talk at her. I knew her mama and daddy.

Susan's parents at their wedding, courtesy of the Henry family.

My daddy and her daddy were seamen. They used to work on the same ship in Saudi Arabia. One time, her daddy fell into the water and was drowning and so my daddy threw a *salvavidas*, a life preserver, and took him out of the water. I used to tell her about all that.

S: What was y'all's relationship like as boyfriend and girlfriend?

A: At the beginning, I just watched her to see if there was something that she needed. I said, "The first present I will give her is a pair of slippers." Yeah, so I gave them to her and she liked them.

S: How did her mom feel about you?

A: She didn't like me. I used to be all over the city and they thought I would never settle down with one girl. They probably thought she deserved a man who had money. A rich person.

In 1989, I moved to the States. We would see each other when I came home, and we got married a year later. In 1991, you were born.

S: All right. How did you like living in New Orleans?

A: I came when I was 23. My father died in 1978 at sea. My mama met my stepfather and they got married. He was an American citizen, so he applied for us with my mama. After that, my four brothers and I came over here.

My first job was on the Mississippi Queen, a tourist boat, as a dishwasher. I was only making $3.15 an hour. We were traveling from here to St. Paul, Minnesota on the Mississippi River. I was there for three months. After that, I flew from St. Paul to Denver, and from Denver, I flew home to get married.

I had a cousin who was working repairing dumpsters for a company named Delta in Jefferson Parish by the Huey P. Long Bridge. I asked him if they had something for me to do and talked to their supervisor. I watched my cousin welding. Then I had to take a test, and did well. I've been a welder in the shipyards, an auto mechanic, a painter, and a garbage collector for a day. I do whatever there is to do.

S: Where were you when I was born?

A: Oh, I was here. I was here in New Orleans.

S: How did you feel about being in the States for years knowing that you had a wife and kids in another country?

A: I felt bad, but I had to do it because I was working. I was so lonely but I had to do it because

Susan as a baby with her godmother and parents, courtesy of the Henry family.

you were ready to be born and we had no money over there for her to have what she needed.

S: Who were you closest to from your family?

A: My mama

S: Why?

A: Everybody goes away, but your mother never goes away. Your mother is always there.

S: What is it like to raise children and does it make you think about your childhood?

A: Well, raising everybody is not easy. When they're small, they will never understand, but then they grow up. Sometimes you want to be old, but when you get old, you don't want to be old anymore.

When I was growing up, my father used to—what do you call those horses? We didn't have a car. He used to work pulling stuff, a *carreta*.

S: Like wagons.

A: He used to pull it with a horse. He moved furniture for people. After that, he got two taxicabs and he used to work in the airport in La Ceiba. In 1974, we had a Hurricane over there—Fifi. Well, we were staying in La Julia, and only one taxi survived. The other one was full of mud. After that, he decided he wanted to be a seaman. I think he went to Panama and from Panama he wanted to sail home and build his own house in Honduras, but he didn't have enough money.

He was working for Zapata Gulf and they merged with Gulf Fleet. A lot of his friends went home, but he decided to go to Saudi Arabia to help put his oldest son through college. He was there for 13 months and the day before he was going home, the sea was rough, and he was trying to jump from one boat to another. Sometimes they come together and then they separate. He tried to jump, he dropped in the middle, and the boats crashed on him. Yeah, he was just 35 years old. My daddy was young, yeah.

S: How do you feel about my mom doing hair?

A: Oh man, she was one of the best in La Ceiba. I used to walk around with your mom and everybody used to holla at her. Everybody wanted her to compete for Miss La Ceiba. She was so beautiful.

S: They told her she couldn't because of the neighborhood she came from— I guess because the neighborhood was too poor.

A: Yeah, but she was Miss La Isla, one of the neighborhoods in La Ceiba, for Carnival.

La Julia

My grandmother was known by everyone in La Julia. Many of my aunts' and uncles' friends call her mom. She calls me *mi reina*, my queen. She'll wake up in the morning and fix my cereal. When she bakes, I sneak into the kitchen to steal the caramels off the cakes.

My grams told me her dad was white and she never met him. She had a harsh childhood taking care of her brothers and sisters. Living with her husband later was worse. He got drunk and beat her. He was a very jealous man, but my mom loved him to death. She always ran to him if Grams stopped to talked to a man. My mom told me Grams threw a curse on her, saying that one day she would have kids and pay for all she did.

My grandmother ended up leaving my grandfather. I only saw him once. He moved from the island of Roatán to La Ceiba and the family he left behind years ago took care of him. My grams didn't want to see him, but she paid for his one-bedroom apartment in La Julia.

My Aunt Jackie brought me to meet him one afternoon when she was dropping off some juice. He was sitting on the bed and asked, "Who is this?" Jackie said, "This is Susan's oldest child."

He said, "So you're Susan's daughter. You're pretty." He looked like he wanted to get up but instead he reached out to me, and said, "Come and give me a hug." When I put my arms around him, I could feel how thin he was. I got to know was how he looked, but not who he was.

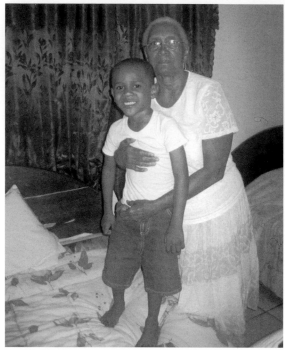

My grandmother had met someone else years ago, my step-granddaddy Eddy, but he died of cancer. He smoked too much. When he died, my grandmother was so sad she wanted to go in the casket with him. I never saw him being disrespectful to her. In front of their house, they ran a small corner store that looked like a snoball stand. They sold homemade bread, burgers, fried pork chops with fried plantains, and coco and Kool-Aid frozen cups. Back in the day, they also sold liquor, but after Eddy died, Grams became a Christian and stopped selling it.

My grams started going to a Spanish-speaking church in La Julia. The church was made of cement. No carpets. The congregation was humble and people didn't really worry about dressing up, except on special occasions. It suited my grams because she didn't put herself above other people.

Interview with My Uncle Earl Henry Brooks, Part I

My uncle Henry is my mother's favorite brother, but I was very afraid of him growing up. We spent a lot of time around each other because I lived with my grams in La Julia and he had an apartment on the property.

My uncle Henry has a strong presence and loves joking around. But he's also very sensitive and protective of the family. When I was little, I thought he was too strict on me and tried to act like he was my daddy. I distanced myself from him so he wouldn't get mad.

When I heard he was coming to New Orleans, I was not happy at all. I thought he might be coming to ruin my life. My mom and grams told me to chill out. When he arrived, he was a totally different person, or maybe I had grown up more. I wanted him to tell me his childhood stories. Talking to him made memories of La Ceiba come back to me.

Uncle Henry, by Susan Henry.

Susan: Where were you born and raised?

Henry: I was born and raised in Honduras, Central America in a small town next to La Ceiba called Atlantida.

S: Where did you live before La Ceiba? You lived in Roatán, right?

H: Yeah, it's a small island—one of the most beautiful places in the world. Actually, there's three islands in the bay, but this is the best one. I wish I could be there right now.

S: How was your childhood?

H: Can I say anything?

S: Yeah, you can say everything.

H: My childhood was really hard. At eight years old, I started working because we weren't getting sufficient money. It was seven of us. I don't like to remember that. As soon as I left school, I started cleaning people's yards and running errands to help my mom. She used to work in a club as a waitress. After she left the club, she came home, washed clothes, and started baking to put food on the table. There were many years that I didn't see my mom because she was working so hard.

The neighborhood where I grew up, Barrio La Julia, is really dangerous. I mean, the young kids do so many drugs and things get out of control.

S: What was it like speaking English in Honduras?

H: We don't have a Spanish last name. Actually, my roots are from England. We live in a Spanish country, but my mom and pop, they're not Spanish. My maternal grandmother, Maggie Bolton, came from Belize to La Ceiba to have a better life. She was a seamstress. From the time that I was little, I remember myself speaking English.

S: How do you feel about speaking Spanish? What language is more comfortable for you?

H: Some words I don't know in Spanish and some words I don't know them in English. Sometimes I mix them up. I think both are comfortable.

S: What was it like growing up black in Honduras?

H: Growing up black in Honduras was a little difficult, because most of the Spanish people there who got their clear color think they're better than you and used to diss you. It was a little bit racist back then. I mean, they used to call you funny names when I was little, right? Like, "black from the devil" and all that stupidness. Actually, my first girlfriend was Spanish. It was a little bit complicated, because the father didn't accept me.

S: How would you describe our culture and how we are different from other people in Honduras? Because I know being mixed with Indian and Spanish and English, we are a little bit different from the other people.

H: All right. I'm gonna put it like this. Spanish people, they always think they're the best, right? But we have four different languages spoken back home.

We got the people, like us, who speak English. There are people who speak Garifuna. The Mosquitos have their own indigenous language. And then we have people who only speak Spanish. Depending on the language that you talk and the color you got on your skin, people are gonna look at you differently. But as soon as they know you're from the United States—or another wealthier country—they're gonna look at you like you're Jesus. The discrimination now is more about money.

S: Some think that you come over here to pick up the money. They don't know the struggle that you go through to work.

H: Everybody thinks it's easy, but when they come over here they see the real life. But over here, I feel much better about my color. Nobody's dissing.

S: How was your relationship with Grandma?

H: I love my mom a lot, but she always wants to be protecting you too much. Mothers do that a lot. She used to tell me that I'm too young to be working, but I'd tell her, "It hurt me more to know that you're hungry and you're stressing." She wanted me to finish primary school.

S: How about your dad? Were you all close?

H: I never got a chance to grow up beside my father. We were living in a house in Roatán. He sold the house and took off with another woman. He left my mom and my other brothers in the street when I was five years old. We didn't know where to go. I never forgave him about that. It was really hard.

When I was 16 years old, I was working and saved

800 *lempiras* to go and look for my father on Roatán with my older brother. That was the first time I'd get the chance to see how he looked.

He was in a *cantina*, like in a bar. He was all drunk. He was looking at me and I was looking at him. I didn't know he was my father until my brother told me. He was smelling bad. I was real clean. He started saying, "Why you bring your brother over here to see me in this condition?" He started getting mad at my older brother.

He was hugging me and calling me son. I was saying, "Why you calling me son and you wasn't there for me?" We started arguing, things got out of control, and I just walked away.

I started seeing him more often. I was trying to give him a position in life. I mean, to call him father. I tried, but I didn't feel it, so I just dropped it and came back to my mother. When my father passed away, I didn't even cry. By that time, I was living in New York.

S: That's how I felt. I met him days before he died. I hugged him, but I didn't—

H: You didn't feel anything.

S: I didn't feel anything, but I felt sorry for him.

H: He used to drink too much. That's why. He didn't eat good, sleep good, nothing— just drinking and drinking.

S: Were you the oldest?

H: Nah, one of the youngest.

S: Were you close to your siblings?

H: I used to love all of my brothers, but with your mom, she was like my best friend.

S: How did you feel about her taking your clothes and making dresses out of them?

H: I felt like punching her face. [*Laughter*] Out of my small shirts, she used to make short pants. I used to be mad and tell my mother, but she wouldn't listen. Afterwards, she'd buy it again or bring me something that I really liked.

S: It's hard talking about my mama. When I was little, it was different.

H: I remember when your mother—she was my sister—but she was beautiful. My sister, damn man, she was beautiful. I've still got pictures.

S: She wanted to be Miss La Ceiba.

H: I saw a lot of people that were hating on her. They didn't give your mother the chance. The people with money said she's black and comes from a bad, bad neighborhood. They said she wasn't gonna look good for our country. That was like really, really painful for everybody, and for her. I remember that.

S: That's kind of different over here, too, because if you make it from small, that's like really something people look up to more.

H: And your mother, nobody taught her. She was born like a model.

S: As I was growing up, I always wanted to be like her.

H: I remember when you were born, there were

Near La Ceiba, courtesy of the Henry family.

seven of us living in a house. It was a small house and you cried a lot.

S: I don't remember.

H: You used to be screaming like crazy and I used to have to go to work—oh man!

S: Tired.

H: And I used to hug you, because your mom—I don't know. She used to be tired, too. I used to take you outside and walk all night with you. You used to be hungry and I put my finger in your mouth, and you used to be sucking my finger. [*Laughter*] That's crazy.

S: When I was small, we used to go to the beach to have picnics.

H: In the summer, yeah. In the summer, it's a *semana santa*.

S: Holy week. I know how to say it in Spanish, but not in English. When Jesus rises—*Pascua*, yeah, Easter.

H: Even the air feels different. It feels clean. Over here in the States, you just work. Sometimes I don't even know the difference when it's morning, afternoon or night. You don't get the chance to—I don't know. It's hard for me to explain. In La Ceiba, when you wash your clothes, you do it in your hand.

S: You hang it outside.

H: And the sun dries it. You cook your food in *estufa de lodo*, in *fogata con madera*.

S: In natural fires.

H: And the food, you take the time to cook properly.

S: It's fresh. When my grandma used to cook,

she'll be like, "Go get me some milk," and I'll go get some milk at one of the corner stores. Or she'll be like, "Go get me some cheese," and I'll go get some cheese, bread, or some fried beans. You don't even have to go grocery shopping—you just go to the corner store and get everything.

H: I remember this man used to get up four a.m. and take the milk from the cow to serve it in the morning.

S: And they have snoballs. They have little carts with ice and they scrape it into a cone, and put the condensed milk on top of it. Tell me a story about me being young and you being little.

H: One day, I whipped you and my other nephew because—

S: We were smoking paper.

H: You rolled it and were smoking. I saw you under the house. It's like a crazy neighborhood. You see that 24/7 —people smoking, drinking.

You were really smart in school. You talked like a grown-up person. All the kids used to be playing with toys and you were trying to do something, *producir algo.*

S: Producing.

H: Yeah, producing stuff—like learning how to do your hair.

S: Take my mama's stuff and get in trouble.

H: Putting makeup all over your face, cutting your hair.

S: I used to do that?

H: Yeah, perm your hair, too, when you were little. Your mama used to be screaming, "What you doin?" I'd tell her, "She want to be like you."

S: And what got you started barbering?

H: Trying to put food on the table.

S: You also said about how my mama always showed you how to do it.

H: I used to see your mother. Everybody in the neighborhood looked for your mother. After she finished working, I saw her counting her money. I said, "Damn, that's good. She makes good money so I'm gonna start looking into it."

Grams Comes to Visit

We lived in my father's mother's house in Englishtown. It was a two story house split into two apartments downstairs and one big house upstairs. We lived on the bottom floor and when my grams, Elenor, came to visit, she stayed upstairs with her husband and her teenage sons, my uncles Cregg and Erick. They dribbled basketball on the hardwood floors and played video games. My mom cooked *machuca,* a fish soup, and everyone loved her recipe.

On Sundays, my grams went to an English-speaking Baptist church called the Church of God in La Isla. My mom would do her hair and then sometimes the three of us would go together. The outside was filled with flowers and bushes. From the front door there was a burgundy carpet leading down to the alter. Microphones and speakers set up for the choir with a keyboard, drum kit, and guitars in front. The curtains were pretty and fancy. The walls didn't have dirt marks. It was very uplifting listening to the gospel music. But after a while, my mom stopped going because some of the women were uppity and looked to see what other people were wearing. My grams loved to dress up for church, so it was never a problem for her.

Beauty Salon

My dad bought a car in the States, sent it on a ship to La Ceiba, and sold it to help my mom start a beauty salon at our house. She was always packed with clients from all over La Ceiba—black, Spanish, she was good at doing all kinds of hair. Sometimes she would be working until two in the morning and I fell asleep watching her. Sometimes I held the combs, hair spray, bobby pins, and anything else she needed. I watched her do "soft" styles from loose curls to flat-irons and "hard" styles from updos to tight curls.

A seamstress rented an apartment on the first floor of my house. She was in her early 50s, heavy set with long, wavy black hair and light skin. She gave me left over fabrics and I made clothes out of them for my baby dolls. I watched her sew pants, skirts, and suits in her living room. Scraps of fabric covered the floor, and couch. Clothes already made were set aside on the dining room table.

One time, she asked me if there was anything she could do about her curls. I told her I could put a relaxer in her hair and that would help with the frizz. My mom saw that some of her supplies were missing and became upset. Maybe because I was giving away our business for free.

A Little Sister

When I was seven years old, my mom became pregnant again. I remember she was always smiling. She had crochet needles and white and green yarn and made a lot of beautiful table decorations for our family while still doing hair.

I was small and didn't really know what was going on, but I wished for a little sister. The day she went into the hospital, she had fainted. The doctors told her the baby was not ready and to come back the next day. When she got home, she wasn't feeling too good so my grandma came over and they headed back to the hospital.

I remember my grandma getting home, saying the baby was born dead. They named her Celine. She went and paid someone to make a small, white coffin. The next day we had the funeral. I got close enough to my sister's face, her light brown skin. My mom was still in the hospital when she was buried. When she came home, she said she held the baby for awhile and then she was gone. I don't know where she is buried. Even though my mom shared stories about me being jealous of her, I remember having plans for us. Of course, I wanted to play in her hair.

Alston Emmanuel

Alston Emmanuel, courtesy of the Henry family.

The doctors told my mother to rest, and to wait to have another baby, but within the same year, she was pregnant again.

All I remember about the day my brother was born was being excited. I remember being in a car with my parents. I sat in the back with my grams, and held Emmanuel. He was so beautiful. He was yellow and his eyes were closed. He had a tiny nose, hair on his head, and his cheeks were red.

After my brother was born, my mom was on bed rest. She took care of the baby and I helped a lot. She would breast feed him and keep him clean and smelling sweet. I thought about it being me as a baby. The only thing I hated was cleaning up his poop.

My dad went back to the States after three months. He started to hear that my mom wasn't acting like herself. She ran my grams from our house saying, "Get out of my house and don't come back." My grams humbly said to her, "Okay, I will never set foot back in your house."

My dad rushed back to check on her, and decided with my mom's family, that she couldn't take care of Emmanuel on her own. They gave him to my Aunt Peach in Roatán. He took his first steps over there. Our cousins, Catty and Edgard, became attached to him, and were sad when he came back to us.

They Called It Depression

At first, I blamed my dad. I figured him being away for so long was hard for her. How could she take not talking to him every day? Not seeing him for, sometimes, more than two years? Wondering what he's doing. Being lonely. When he surprised us by coming home, she didn't know how to act.

When she wasn't doing well, she would spend most of her time sleeping. My dad sent us money from the States, and she gave it all to me. I bought toys and unnecessary things but also school supplies and food. I looked after my brother, and he started to call me "Mom." I always got upset for that.

Our family called it depression. She had an urge to break and ruin things. She burned family pictures in the backyard, broke tons of dishes, threw away clothes, and gave away house appliances. She told her sisters they envied her and always did. She told my grandmother that she knew she never forgave her for always telling her dad about her. She claimed my grams had a favorite daughter and it wasn't her.

She cut all her hair off and sometimes she wouldn't even wear shoes. She fought with her brothers and sisters. One time I saw my uncle Henry holding her down as she fought back. She hid knives under the bed and sometimes carried them around. Sometimes she would just sit there and not make a sound. She wouldn't eat. Seemed like she took all her frustration out on me. I told her,

Why do you do this?
You don't love anyone
You don't care
La odio

She also told me the same things. I didn't want to fear her, but I did. I didn't want to hate her, but I did. I wish I never blamed God, but I did.

"God, if you are real, heal her. I'm too young to be a mother."

It was just her, Emmanuel, and me at home. I had no one to help me watch over her. She didn't want her family around. She ran out of the house at midnight, leaving me alone with my brother. I was scared to follow her. One time, her brother found her and she had spots of blood on her dress. I didn't know where it came from.

Sometimes when she needed me, I wouldn't be brave enough to say, "I'm here for you" or "I love you."

I grew up not saying, "I love you." The words weren't in my vocabulary. That was fine with me. I didn't realize I could be hurting my little brother. He didn't have someone to say, "I love you" to him. I was too tough to say it.

When is This Day Coming?

I always knew I was coming to the States since I was a little girl. My grams Elenor visited and would remind me that my dad would bring us. I had no idea of what was to come. I watched the T.V. shows and thought my life would turn in to something like that. I mentioned to my friends that I was leaving but they never believed me. It took so long. They asked, "When is this day coming?"

"In some months...in a year...not this year, but next year." The days changed. My best friend Pamela lived down the street. She was white with long, Indian looking hair. We both had family in the States that would send us boxes, but her aunt had crossed through the back and couldn't send for her the same way that my dad could for me. A typical conversation between us would go:

Me: Barbies over in the States are less expensive.

Pamela: I know, my aunt sends some when she sends boxes over.

Me: When I leave, I'll try to call you every day.

Pamela: Are you staying with your grams?

Me: Until we get a house of our own.

Pamela: Are you ever coming back?

Me: Probably to visit.

The first time my dad signed for our papers, my mother burned her passport, birth certificate, and other important documents. I knew they were important because he had to pay a lot of money, and we had to go to San Pedro to take a physical and a drug test to get them. We had already been waiting for three years and my dad had to start all over again.

The day before we left Honduras, my grandmother and all of my aunts came over to help us clean and pack up. When it got close for us to leave, I cried. My grams whispered in my ear, "It's all over," Those words I'll never forget. I believed her. She was happy believing so, too.

On the plane, my dad and I sat together and my mom and brother sat behind us. I had never felt so much joy being with my parents. I thought everyplace would be like New York City—big buildings and celebrities everywhere. I thought we would have a big house for the four us and we'd all have Christmas together.

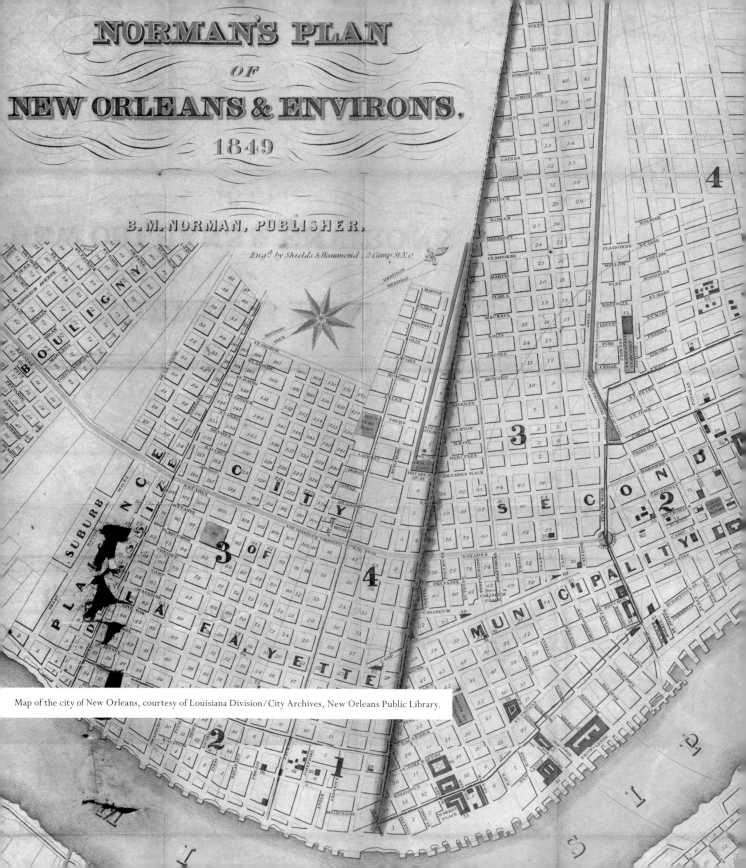

Map of the city of New Orleans, courtesy of Louisiana Division/City Archives, New Orleans Public Library.

Part II: New Orleans

Susan's grandparents' house on Paris Avenue, by Susan Henry.

The Day I Came to the States

I didn't know where I was because I was so dizzy from all the throwing up I did. I threw up on the plane, and in the truck. I closed my eyes and tried to stay calm and go to sleep.

When I woke up, we were turning onto Paris Avenue, parked in front of a big white house with blue trim. It was pretty, but it wasn't what I imagined. My grams' house in La Ceiba was so beautiful that I thought she'd be living in a mansion.

My dad and his brother unloaded the bags from my uncle's truck. I grabbed one bag and we headed to the door. My dad opened it. I was nervous. I had pictures in my head of the whole family being there to welcome us. We walked in and the first person I saw was my grams folding towels in the kitchen. I hugged her and ran into the bathroom to take a shower because I had throw up on my shirt. My mom made me change into a dress and we went to my uncle Harys' house on the Westbank. His house was a two story, four bedroom house. The first floor was made of bricks and the second had vinyl siding. I was impressed, but shy the whole time. My cousin Nikky had some friends over and everyone was wearing jeans. My old long dress felt huge and out of place.

My Aunt Jen drove us to Walgreens. She gave me 20 bucks but I didn't know what to buy so I just kept the money. It was the most American money I'd ever had.

Nikky

My cousin came to the States when she was a baby. She has beautiful green eyes and dirty blonde natural hair. When I met her, she loved wearing jeans and flip flops. Heels, sometimes, but not too high and just for church. She talked me into doing her chores around the house since I was faster at folding laundry. She was the big sis I never had.

Nikky and Susan, courtesy of the Henry family.

We had sleep overs on the weekends and stayed up all night. I did her hair or we snuck out to go swimming in her backyard. We told each other everything and never cared how gross, embarrassing, or painful the memories were. Her brother Sean fussed with us because we talked in Spanish and he couldn't understand us.

When we went to Walmart, and spent all of our money buying makeup and acrylic nails. At home, we spread everything on the bed and played with it. One time we tried to shoplift together and we almost got caught. We ran out of Walmart and into my grams' car. Every time we saw a police car, we got scared and looked at each other.

We knew each other better than anyone. Sometimes I envied her a little. I felt she had a perfect life and didn't appreciate it. Sometimes I wanted what she had and felt like my grams liked her better. I first got that idea from the fact that my grams never baked me a cake for my birthday, but when Nikky's birthday was coming up, she would bake her a cake and sometimes bring it over herself. She would complain about being tired, but she would still get it done.

One time I wrote my grams a letter mentioning the way I felt about her never showing any type of excitement towards my birthday. I slid it under the bathroom door while she was taking a shower. After she read it, she called me up to her room and said that wasn't true and gave me 20 bucks and said, "Happy birthday." Another year passed by, but still no cake.

Nikky's parents found out she was talking to boys, and she moved to Honduras to stay with her mother. We cried till we were out of tears.

Susan and her cousins celebrating a birthday, courtesy of the Henry family.

Different

Having a different background and accent to go with it was not easy in elementary school. I got teased a lot. My mom spoke English to me since I was young. It was my first language despite growing up in Honduras where most people spoke Spanish. I used think my mama was preparing me to live in the States.

I always thought there was just one type of English, but when I moved to New Orleans, I saw how many there were. In school, I got put down one grade. They thought I didn't know enough English because I came from another country, even though I could always understand the lessons. For one period of the day, they also put me in an English as a Second Language class. It was just me, a teacher, and a desk.

Kids would ask me to say certain words they knew I couldn't pronounce, like "three." And I'd say, "tree." They cracked up and I didn't know what they were laughing at. I couldn't hear the difference. Sometimes when we'd write notes to pass in class, I would spell words the way they sounded to me and the other kids would laugh.

Susan and Emmanuel on Paris Avenue.

I was so quiet, it was hard to find people to hang out with. I looked different from the other girls and acted different, too. I've always been really thin and the girls in my school had a lot more curves. The boys teased me because I was really skinny, and the girls felt superior with their big butts and boobs.

Now when people at school ask me where I'm from, I know they mean what hood. In elementary, I always answered Honduras or Central America. I didn't know any better. I told my uncle Cregg about it and he laughed and said, "Dawg, just say you from the Seventh Ward."

Felipe Smith, by Lindsey Darnell.

Interview with Felipe Smith, Part I

When I moved into the Seventh Ward, I didn't know any-thing about the neighborhood. Paris Avenue was quiet and it hasn't changed much since the storm. Nobody's outside. We don't know our neighbors' names. I don't know their background. If they've ever heard my grandparents speak, they would know we weren't from here, but they don't talk long enough. My classmates say "I'm black" or "I'm African American."

I heard the word Creole being used in Honduras to describe my family but never knew what it meant. As a child, I grew up not paying attention to my background and where my family was from. I took for granted that my dad and his family were in the States. I didn't know why. I just wanted us to be together.

I decided to talk to Felipe Smith, a professor of African Diaspora Studies at Tulane University about the Seventh Ward and La Ceiba. Felipe was born in New Orleans, but his people are from Englishtown. He inherited their ways, although it took him a long time to understand his history. I wanted to interview him because I thought we had a lot in common. Even though he was born in New Orleans, he had to adjust to a different way of living because his parents were immigrants. It helped me because during the interview I learned a lot of things not only about the West Indian community in Honduras, but also the history of the Sev-enth Ward, the neighborhood I have lived in since I moved to New Orleans.

The United Fruit Company steamship that traveled from La Ceiba, Havana, and New Orleans, courtesy of Felipe Smith.

Susan: Will you tell me about your family history?

Felipe: My family's history is complicated because it's partially Hispanic and partially Anglophone English-speaking Caribbean. My father's grandmother was from Belize and she migrated to Honduras around the turn of the century with a large influx of English speaking people into Honduras because of the banana agriculture that was then beginning to be a big employment industry in the area. My mother's parents also migrated for the same reason but from a different direction. My maternal grandmother was born in Panama, but they were originally Jamaican and Cayman Islanders who identified as West Indians but migrated around Central American whenever work was available.

Then in the 1940s and 50s, they began to migrate into the United States—some on the East Coast up to New Jersey and New York. My branch of the family wound up here because my father was at the time working for United Fruit Company. He was born in Chamelecón, which is more interior than my mother's birthplace in La Ceiba. He eventually moved to La Ceiba. He and my mother actually went to school together as kids. At some point, they were in English school because the Anglophone community there had its own schools but they also went to the regular schools where they were taught in Spanish. I think the English school was a subscription school, which meant that they had to pay to go to it.

I have a picture of United Fruit Company steamship in the harbor in Havana. The ship would go to La Ceiba, pick up bananas go to Havana and then it would come here from Havana. Havana and New Orleans were actually very closely connected before the embargo in the 1960s. But it wasn't just that my father was sailing on that ship that it became meaningful to me. It was the ship that my mother came across from Honduras on with my sister. It had passenger quarters as well as it was a merchant ship

Photo by Charles Franck Studio. Courtesy The Historic New Orleans Collection, Acc. no. 1979.325.3574.

carrying produce. My whole family experience has to do with that connection to Cuba—the stopping off point between Central America and New Orleans.

When I was in Cuba, I met West Indians who had come over for the same reasons my parents moved to Honduras. They are very formal. They are very proper. Everything has to be done in a certain way. Growing up, I didn't see that as being West Indian. I saw that as being Honduran. I didn't have the frame to understand it. Part of my greater understanding of self has come through exploring those kinds of situations and getting a better sense of my own family history and how that shaped me. I'm still on that journey. I don't see it ending any time in the near future.

S: My family has the Roatán to La Ceiba/English-town connection, too.

F: So your family was based on Roatán?

S: On my mother's side, yes.

F: Right and why did they move? Do you know?

S: On my mother's side, my grandmother moved when she separated from my grandfather. She moved to La Ceiba. I just started to figure out stuff.

F: And how old were you when you came here?

S: Ten.

F: Ten, okay. I don't know if your parents are like mine, but they were very reluctant to just volunteer information if asked. They would volunteer information if not asked—largely in a context where they were trying to prove a point or chastise you. But if you asked them something, they would clam up and get very defensive, "Why do you want to know that?" We just gradually developed the attitude that they're sensitive about where they come from.

We were living in the Seventh Ward, on New Orleans Street between Miro and Galvez, which was the Creole community historically. There were families that had long periods of residence here. You got to be known by whether your family was a known family or whether you were an unknown. If you were an unknown, you had to have gotten here by some means that other people recognized as being a part of a traditional or a historical pattern of moving into the neighborhood. It was a very complex kind of social space. I think my parents just gradually grew very defensive about having to account for who they were and why they were here and they reflected that with our conversations with them.

In New Orleans, my father worked for United Fruit Company and then for Lykes Brothers, which was a shipping concern that took over a lot of the United Fruit Company shipping lanes in the Gulf. The ship would be gone for three weeks and then back in New

Orleans on a regular routine—that's why he stayed with the company that took over the ship. He was a cook. He worked his way up from being just a kind of regular helper. Then he became a helper in the kitchen, and then he gradually connected with people who taught him how to do basic things and from there he advanced to becoming the first cook.

My mother was a housekeeper and a maid. She worked in a number of different households while we were growing up and even beyond when we were growing up. She worked to have extra money that was under her control. If there was anything that she needed or thought somebody else needed, she would do what was called in those days "day work." In some cases, it was a regular job. In other cases, it was on-call and you basically signed up to work for that day. It paid an incredibly small amount of money and it was a kind of work that was very much connected to the slave traditions of the past.

When I was growing up in the 1950s and 60s, it was possible for people that had lower-middle income levels to have household maids. I had high school friends whose mothers worked as maids in very modest houses. It was possible for these households because unskilled black women workers, who had no other income opportunities given the segregated nature of education and of the types of jobs that you could actually get, would work all day—and I mean from eight in the morning until ten at night for sometimes five to ten dollars a day and whatever leftovers the person might decide to give them.

My mother would get on the bus in the morning at six in the morning and not come back until sometimes 11 at night. At the end of the week, she might

Felipe's father, Felipe Smith Lazo, courtesy of Felipe Smith.

have 40 dollars that she didn't have before. It was a strange situation to be in. We were living in a fairly middle class neighborhood in the Seventh Ward and yet this was not an unusual thing for people's mothers to do.

S: What was it like in the Seventh Ward?

F: We had a block with something like upwards of 50-70 kids. This was the Baby Boom era. A small family would have had five children. It was a culture where parents were working or overwhelmed. Kids would get thrown outside until as long as they could stay out and we basically socialized ourselves through our interaction with peer groups as opposed to now where families will have one or two children and they'll allot more parenting as the norm. In those days, our lives were organized around what the rest of the neighborhood was involved in. Those times won't come back. Nobody will go back to those six and seven children families anymore.

I went to probably the largest elementary school maybe in the city at the time. I went to Valena C. Jones School—because of its location one of the preeminent schools for black New Orleanians. Valena C. Jones School and Corpus Christi were the two schools that served that community and there was a certain amount of prestige in going to those schools. A typical class might be between 35-40 students. It was ridiculously overcrowded. Part of what was distinctive about being there was that it was overwhelmingly Catholic and yet there was a very strong mostly Baptist, Protestant population in the public school. It was like living in a context where you had these two really defined kinds of spaces where you fit into.

You were either with the predominant sort of Catholic Creole neighborhood or you were a part of this other group—many of whom were more recent arrivals from the area outside of the city. Many of them had Mississippi backgrounds. Just the way people spoke was an indication of what group they fit into because it was almost different languages between those groups. The Creole kids, many of them had French Creole speaking parents or grandparents and so they had that kind of accent that comes from people who are French Creole speaking. The others whose parents were from the country had more of a typically kind of Southern accent—like a Mississippi kind of accent to them. But again there were enough of each of those groups so that they were familiar with each other. They understood how each other spoke.

Felipe's mother, Bernice Hendricks Smith Lazo, courtesy of Felipe Smith.

S: What challenges did your family face as black Hondurans in the 1950s?

F: That's a good question. There were two ways that we kind of complicated things for other people. When we came in, we were a third way of speaking. One of the things that I found out later was the way we spoke had to do with the fact that our family was West Indian. The English that West Indians spoke was more British-influenced than it was American-influenced and so the way certain words were pronounced was very different.

It was like even the parts of our identity which were English were not the English that they were familiar with. For example, my father's given name is Felipe but his friends called him Philip, not "Phil-up" the way it was pronounced with Southerners, but "Phil-ip" which is very British. That was my nickname, too—Philip. But it was complicated for people who were not familiar with that English dialect, so they came up with all sorts of crazy ways of saying that. It created these moments where people would just stand back and say, "Y'all talk funny, y'all act funny, why are y'all so different?"

It creates a certain kind of pressure. Different family members of mine assimilated a lot more. Some of us were more to ourselves, so we had more difficulty in terms of transition. My sister and I were put into speech therapy classes when we were in elementary school because the teachers decided that we had speech impediments because we talked different.

S: That happened to me a lot—well happens to me when I say I'm not from here. People then say, "Oh, I hear your accent." But I have to say I'm not from here first. In fifth grade I used to get pulled out of class to go to English/Spanish speaking class. It'd be like one period and everybody would always be like, "Why do you have to go to that class if you know how to speak English?" But I just had to take it because I'm not from here. It's like I have to take it.

F: So someone looked at your record and basically immediately said, "Oh, well you need this class."

S: Mhm and like another thing they did was when I came here they lowered me down one grade. Like I was supposed to come and immediately be in the 6th grade and they put me in the 5th just because they assumed that I didn't know enough.

F: Did they ever readjust your grades?

S: No, I just kept going on from there.

F: Are you angry about that?

S: Yeah.

F: I would be, too.

S: Did people make stupid sarcastic comments about you not being from here or your family not being from here?

F: Well, growing up in a black community, it's just inevitable that when the ribbing contests start people are going to fasten on whatever it is that's different about you. I grew up in a neighborhood where people were constantly cracking on each other and it was merciless. I was violent as a child as a result of it. I was not thick-skinned enough to take that kind of verbal abuse and so I had only two mentalities. One was I would just be normal and interact with people and then the other personality was I was homicidal and I would just pick up anything and try to hit them with it. I had a bad reputation. People knew that they could go only so far pushing me with that stuff.

S: Did they have any strange ideas about how Hondurans would be like?

F: Yeah, but part of the problem was we didn't really have any good information to correct their misimpressions with because what we knew of the story and what we could see from the pictures was—it didn't quite fit together. We could see pictures of houses and places that my parents lived in that looked like something you would see on a "help the starving children" kind of poster. But my mother would be telling stories of how our grandfather had the largest house in this

A postcard of La Ceiba, courtesy of The Latin American Library, Tulane University.

part of the city and that people were always going to his house whenever they needed a place to stay, that he had huge property holdings in three different cities. She said he had huge property holdings in Roatán. He had a kind of farm plot in Tela that he would go to like periodically and grow crops and then he had a large house in La Ceiba.

Whenever we would ask for clarification, "How could that be when here's a picture of one of my older sisters and she's lying on a bed and in the background is this corrugated tin house?" We were just not getting it. I think it was generational for my parents that you didn't question older people. That was a West Indian thing that I didn't realize until I started dealing with other people who were Jamaican or from Guyana. Also, there were so many of us that we never got to go there. My mother went back in my childhood at least twice and when she went she went alone. My brother, who I didn't meet until I was 5 years old when he came to New Orleans—I was shocked that he spoke English. We were just clueless. In fact, his

experience was slightly different from yours. When he got here, he was so well-spoken that they tried to skip him grades because he just seemed to have a better command of the language. For us, we were self-conscious of it because it was different from the way people talked. It became a point of feeling like outsiders and so we tried to work against it. Whereas when he came, it just sounded a lot more impressive that he had this command of English.

In answer to the question though, most of the kinds of issues that we ran into with other people about Honduras had to do with clothing and food because these were the things that were the most material in the sense that other people would notice them. We would get a hard time about that. "Why do you wear those clothes?" Well, give me an alternative. This is what I was handed and told to wear. Or food—food was really important because people were in and out of each other's houses a lot and people responded to the different stuff.

33

It's always amazing about New Orleans—it's so different than everywhere else, you would think there would be this kind of openness to difference but New Orleanians don't see it as different. Most of the people we knew had a very limited kind of exposure to anything outside of New Orleans. Before the interstate highways were put in, it wasn't on the way to anywhere, so people were really very isolated. We had a sense that New Orleans was not like the rest of the world because we had information coming in to us from people who were in other parts of the world and we had a basis for comparison. Our friends didn't because their whole family and acquaintance universe was centered around New Orleans. It just became like an echo chamber.

S: I can relate to what you were saying about ideas that they had about how it would be over there. Like me, they would ask me, "Do they have McDonald's over there? Do they have Pizza Hut?" And I'm like, "Yes, they do." They'll be shocked. Or like this one time, I had a picture in my journal and this girl at school took it and she was like, "Oh my God you can dress." She as assuming that since I'm not from here that I can't dress and I was like, "Oh my God."

F: One thing I found out when I went to Honduras was that the Coca-Cola is very different.

S: It's good!

F: It doesn't use the same sugar and so there's a very different taste to it.

S: It's good. My dad always used to send me to buy a Coke. Every time my mom would cook I always would get him a Coke.

F: Well, one day I was just walking through this neighborhood and there was a store there. I went and bought a Coke and when the woman understood that I was leaving she poured it in a plastic bag and I was like, "Whoa!" But I guess it was the economics of losing the bottle and not having it to get refilled. We're so used to everything being disposable. But I remember the Pizza Hut there in the downtown area.

S: In Centro? It's still there, too. Did you speak Spanish at home?

F: No. In fact, I'm still not bilingual. I'm still struggling to try to develop some Spanish language skills. My parents were both Anglophone and English was our household language. We knew that they were bilingual but their Spanish speaking was with other adults and in the context of things that children should not know. Some of us tuned out and others tried to learn Spanish to figure out what they were saying. We got words like *pendejo* or *carajo* which I was shocked to find out are actually not vulgar expressions. *Pendejo* means something like idiot. We thought they were really bad.

S: Other than your brother did you have any other brothers or sisters that lived with you that were from Honduras?

F: Yeah half of my immediate family were. My two oldest brothers were left behind in the care of my grandparents and then I had an older sister who was I think maybe two years old when my mother moved to New Orleans. At the time, she was pregnant with my older brother. Then she got my oldest sister to come because she had two small children in the house and decided she needed somebody to help. One of my older brothers died in Honduras before I was born, so that left only my brother who finally came when I was five. The other four of us were born here. My sister was always trying to assimilate—to fit in to what everyone else was doing. My brother was always kind of radical.

When he got to New Orleans, and began to experience racial discrimination—it's not that he was unaware of it growing up in Honduras because there was that element there too—but in the U.S. it was the beginning of the Civil Rights Movement when he arrived. He joined the Nation of Islam and when he did my parents basically said, "You can't stay here because the police would be here and it'll be all kinds of problems." They had the kinds of anxieties that people who are worried about their citizenship status have where they don't want the police around under any context. He went to New York and got into one of the mosques there; I think the one in Harlem when Malcolm X was there. And then he did a complete 180. The next time we made contact with him he was still in New York but he was working as a bus driver. He reconciled with my parents.

S: What kind of food did your family cook?

F: Well, we had maybe the best of both worlds. Working as a housekeeper in households, my mother was periodically asked to do some cooking so she gradually learned how to do the New Orleans stuff. But then she also had the things that were a part of her base culture in coastal Honduras with this West Indian background. Some of the things that they were eating were a part of West Indian diet that was not necessarily Honduran. For example, things like

johnnycakes. I have a lot of West Indian friends who have different formulas for making johnnycakes, but everybody knows how.

S: My mother makes those a lot.

F: Right, I'm going to come by your house. I have gone to New York to get a package of johnnycakes because it's a whole way of life if you've never had the experience. There are things like coconut beans and rice.

S: She makes that, too.

F: Okay, and a lot of plantain type dishes—whether it was baked, fried or using the plantain in soups where you had a lot of yucca and malanga. The incredible thing is that we knew these things because they were sold here. Unbeknownst to us, there was a much larger Honduran community that was familiar with the food. It was very much from that coastal area. I think there was some Garifuna influence as well, although the Garifuna pretty much kept themselves distinct from the West Indians. It was like that with the two different black communities. They had different histories.

We had things like the guava paste. We had lobster with a very great regularity when I was growing up and that was not part of a typical New Orleans type of seafood regimen, which was mostly crawfish and boiled crabs.

Creole, for me, began to be understandable in the context of Creole as a kind of adaptation to the local environment. As these West Indians migrated for work from one place to another, they participated in these Creole types of cultural experiences. What

Above: Felipe's mother and siblings, from left to right: Sidney Smith Lazo, Bernice Hendricks Smith Lazo, Felipe Smith, Andrea Lazo Rice, Avida Raquel Marcea, France Smith Lawless, Ceola Lazo, courtesy of Felipe Smith.

my family was doing would be considered Creole customs—an adaptation to the customs that people had in like the *mestizo* population in Honduras. My mother made tamales. She made tortillas with *masa harina*, but she also had the West Indian food. We thought that was the way everybody from Honduras was and were shocked when we came to understand that the prevalent Honduran identity is something completely different than what we knew as being Honduran.

There were different areas of the city where Hondurans were. For example, closer to Canal Street there were more Honduran and other Hispanic groups. There's a lot of Hondurans in Kenner. They might have realized that their best opportunities had to do with trying to distance themselves from blackness as much as they possibly could—even into the 1970s and 1980s this was true.

The Honduras connection was something that came and went but being in the Seventh Ward was 24/7. When we grew up, we were in and out of the houses

of neighbors, but if the Creole Catholic kids who lived across the street had their cousins visiting, well, we couldn't go to their house because for them it was a class issue. We didn't understand that skin color was associated with class and they didn't want to reflect to their relatives that they were interacting with this lower class element and there were other variations on that. Or, for example, we had a lot of businesses that were owned and operated by Italians, Greeks, Cajuns. So there would be these black neighborhoods but then there would be this white, ethnic family and we were all part of the rabble, but when their relatives showed up—they might show up in an old beat up truck— and all of a sudden they didn't interact with neighborhood kids because that was simply beneath them. Gradually, we learned these codes. Not through people telling us in so many words, but just by the way that our parents would automatically go into defensive behavior patterns.

I remember a conversation where the guy who grew up in the neighborhood with us whose family owned the store was talking about going to school and it occurred to me that he was in the ninth grade just like my brother and I said, "Do you guys ever see each other at school?" And they looked at me like, "What!?" There was this complete quiet because there was no language to describe the mistake that I had made. If they were forced to talk about it, then the whole thing would fall to pieces.

There were large pockets of the Seventh Ward which were occupied by whites and the way you walked through a white neighborhood was different than the way you walked through a Creole neighborhood, which was different from the way you would walk through a black neighborhood. This was all within four or five blocks of my house. I remember being chased out of neighborhoods when I would walk on Broad Street—a border between the white and Creole parts of town. Little kids, six years old, running behind us calling us names, throwing rocks. It was a part of the geography. You knew that when you entered that area there was a higher likelihood of a confrontation. You couldn't leave your own neighborhood without moving from one part of this social spectrum into another. It was like there were all of these invisible lines that you had to know by feel more than anything.

S: In my part, it's very quiet. You don't hardly see people. Before the storm, on Bruxelles, I didn't really see any white people around there and now I don't see anybody at all. Oh, why do you think darker blacks were more discriminated against than lighter skinned blacks?

F: Wow, that one has a long history. In terms of survival, your chances were greater— your opportunities were greater—the more you looked like the dominant group of people. Creoles were more likely to be middle class because they were more likely to have had parents who understood the value of an education because there was actually a payoff to having an education.

A part of this, I think, still explains why a culture of educational accomplishment is still very much something that people don't place a high degree of value in. Many of those communities did not have anecdotal

evidence that it paid off. Their evidence of what paid off had more to do with, "Oh, when you get a certain age you can go work on the docks." Or, "When you get a certain age, you can go work in a hotel."

All of that speaks to the fact that there was a reward system in place for people who were physically closer to the dominant culture ideal. For example, the story that Ernest Morial told about his father being a Creole painter who became white when he crossed Canal Street to go and work on jobs. His complexion was such that they didn't have to know that he was black. There were a lot of Creoles in the city who did not identify themselves as having black ancestry. You could be a Creole and be in this ambiguous position of not looking black and therefore be assumed to be one of the white Creoles and because both communities spoke French Creole as a language it was a kind of area where people could claim that identity and not have to deal with the discrimination that went with being black.

People wonder why there are so many people here under the official poverty level—it is possible to live a fairly comfortable life without having a lot. There is seasonal employment so that people can work very hard for a short period of time whether it's in the seafood industry or the tourist industry and then spend the rest of the year not working and still being able to make it. These are the kinds of anecdotal experiences people had.

Within the sort of larger black community, there were informal and formal ways of distinguishing different groups of people through rituals. For example, the Autocrat Club is now just a kind of social meeting place but in the 1950s and early 60s it was a space that was restricted to Creoles because there were entrance requirements to their activities that were patrolled on the basis of skin color. My sisters were lighter skinned than myself and my two brothers. It just happened that way. We were darker and they were lighter. They could go places that we couldn't go in the same neighborhood. Like we could play on people's porch, but they could go in the house. We had to know that these boundaries existed and why. So it was just ingrained in you.

S: What did you do after graduating from high school?

F: I stayed here and I went to the University of New Orleans (UNO) for four years. I trained as a social studies teacher. I couldn't get a job teaching social studies. I minored in English so I started teaching English. I taught in the public schools for about six years. In 1978, I went back and got a Master's degree in English at UNO and that allowed me to teach at a college level. I was offered a job teaching English at LSU, which I took. I inquired about teaching locally in New Orleans and I was told that I could get a teaching position at UNO, so I stopped teaching at LSU and taught there for two years. I was told that I would not have a permanent job without a doctorate, so I enrolled in the doctoral program at LSU and finished my doctoral degree in 1988. Since then, I've been teaching at Tulane.

S: Where do you live now?

F: I live in New Orleans East. Along with everybody else in my generation, I gradually moved further and further away. When we were becoming adults, there was no real room for expansion in the Seventh Ward.

It was an overcrowded place. People just gradually moved further and further to the East and we wound up moving to Bullard Avenue in 1989. So this is just about 20 years.

S: I'm writing a book and I'm wondering what advice you would give me about other things I should include.

F: I think for you what has to happen is that you have to see yourself in terms of your own personal transformation. This transformation will tell you what's important and what's not important to put in the book—what to give emphasis to based on your own experiences, your journey. It's all about getting a vision of yourself and then trying to color in the spaces in between.

It's important to developing an attitude about the process of being creative. It's like knowing how to translate experience into words about experience— how to pay attention to things as they're going on and to be able to figure out their significance. You have to practice being the interpreter of your own experience. You're always telling yourself the story of yourself in real time. It's like having a second language and you're processing it in two different ways. You're hanging out with your friends but boom, you're also telling yourself the story of hanging out with your friends. Then you will know what makes the story understandable and meaningful to other people. For me, I was able to think of it in terms of having a personal mythology. By putting myself at a distance, I could see myself and then describe myself. I could begin to recognize what other people would need to be able to understand what this story was about.

ESL Class

New Orleans has the largest population of Hondurans outside of Honduras. But I only knew my family. In middle school, I was put in an ESL class all day long. There were six other students: a brother and sister who were born here, but whose family was from Mexico, two brothers from Chile, a boy from Guatemala, and three of us from La Ceiba.

Omar had dark skin and curly soft hair. You could tell he wasn't from the States because he wore his pants tight around his waist. The others girls in the school liked him, but I didn't. In our small class, Leo used to tease me and say, "Susan and Omar, sitting in the tree. K-i-s-s-i-n-g."

I was the only black girl. Once again, I was different, but it didn't feel so bad because we were all learning a new culture together.

At lunch, we spoke Spanish and the other students thought we were talking about them and sometimes we were. After school, we walked to the bus stop together and sometimes the two other girls and me went shopping on Canal Street. We had a different sense of style than the New Orleans girls—I think we were the only ones that were crazy about heels. One dress-down day at school, we all wore tight jeans, blouses, and black boots. Everyone said we were cute.

Interview with My Grams, Elenor Watler

My grandmother's name is Elenor Watler. She's known me since I was a baby but I didn't remember her until we met when I was eight years old. She brought me shoes, skirts and dresses from the States to go to church. She's outspoken, caring, spiritual, strict, and a clean freak. She doesn't wear short sleeve shirts, jeans, shorts, or skirts about the knee.

After a few years in the States, I became real close with my grandmother. I told her everything. I helped her around the house and fixed her hair for church. She called me up to her room to watch shows about surgeries and natural disasters on the Discovery Channel or the Spanish news.

My grams is good in the kitchen. She used to cook three times a week, but now that she works at Walmart, it's more like every other Sunday. When she does, I'll wake up in the middle of the night for a third plate.

I usually talk to my grams about day to day life. I'll play with her all day. Sometimes my uncle Cregg will help me. My mama says, "You need to stop playing with yo grandma like that." And I'll be like, "That's not my grandma, that's my best friend. Tell her, Grams." She laughs and tells me to fold clothes.

She also tells me, "You better not have no boyfriend."

She thinks that boys these days aren't serious. They just want to have fun with girls and leave them when they get pregnant. I tell her, "Man, it's stupid when grown folks tell their children stuff like that cause then they just sneak and do it. I'ma let you know. I'll even bring him to the house, me."

"I'ma beat him up."

"Well, I'ma take the chance."

As close as we are, I didn't know that much about my grams' background. She usually told me stories when she wanted to make me feel guilty about my lifestyle or that she had it harder growing up than me. I'd tell her, "You didn't have the same life as me, so why are you bugging me about it?" She always said, "You young children..." And I'd think, "Oh, Lord! Here she goes again." So this interview was my chance to hear stories that tell me more about the reasons why she is so conservative. I wanted to know about her experiences in Honduras, but also what it's been like to live far away from home and her experiences as a black Honduran woman in New Orleans.

Elenor Watler, by Lindsey Darnell.

Susan: We are in the Seventh Ward and I'm interviewing my grandmother Elenor. Grandma, where are you from?

Elenor: Honduras, Central America. Roatán Bay Island. I left when I was very young.

S: Why did y'all move to La Ceiba?

E: Roatán, at the time, was poor. There wasn't any jobs there. My mama took us to—we call it—the Mainland looking for better living for us.

S: Where did you live in La Ceiba?

E: In Englishtown. The black people used to go to Englishtown to live. We speak more English and they named it Englishtown.

S: How is La Ceiba different from other parts of Honduras?

E: It's different because there are a lot of people from the Bay Islands in La Ceiba, and most of them are descended from Cayman and Jamaica that was controlled by the British. That's the reason why we speak English, because our ancestors came from those islands, and they reside there in Roatán, Honduras. In other parts of Honduras, there's not a lot of black people. La Ceiba has the most black people. It's a beautiful place to visit, to live.

S: What was it like being English speaking and of mixed descent in Honduras?

E: We speak both languages—Spanish and English—and we had advantages over people who only spoke one. But it was a lot of discrimination from the light-skinned Spanish people towards us. We didn't mix much when I was growing up. We lived near each other, but a black person usually didn't marry a Spanish person. They just throw the "n" word in your face. It's better now.

S: Did you go back to Roatán?

E: Yes, I went back when I was about 14 years old to visit. To know the place where I was born was nice—to meet family that I didn't know. I don't know too much about my daddy's family because I grew up mostly around my mama's family, yeah. They all remembered me. My mama's parents were from Cayman. My grandmother had sisters there and

41

A postcard of La Ceiba, courtesy of The Latin American Library, Tulane University.

she used to go visit her family. My grandfather had a little boat and he traveled from village to village on the island, yes. It's 36 miles long. He used to raise cows and other animals. He also had gardens with watermelons. He sold what he raised around the island. I also went back in June 2009.

S: You ain't tell me that!

E: Now it's a lot of different people—a lot of stores. When I was growing up there, they had one car—an old truck from the government—and one straight street. But now a lot of money is going in there and so many other streets that have opened up.

S: How did you meet my dad's dad?

E: We met at church. I've been going to the Church of God in La Isla, a neighborhood in La Ceiba, since I was 16 years old.

S: Why did you get married so young?

E: My mama died and left nine of us. My daddy had abandoned us. We didn't have nowhere to stay. I had a little sister who was six years old and I had to take care of her. I married when I was 17 and had someplace to live with my sister.

S: Why did your husband go to sea?

E: Because he was looking better living for the children. We didn't had the money that we needed to put our children through school and that's why he went to sea.

S: How did you feel about him being a seaman?

E: I didn't want him to do it because it was a dangerous job, but that was the only way he could make a living—going up there and providing for us.

S: How was it like to have a long distance relationship? You know, because my mama and daddy had a long distance relationship when he was working over here.

E: I got used to it. We talked over the phone and when his ship came on in the port there in Puerto Cortez, I went down to meet him.

S: How did my dad take his death?

E: He took it hard. He was very close to his daddy. He would go sit in his lap when he came back from sea. He missed his daddy a lot. I was 30. It was a real hard time in our life back home. I was doing laundry for people.

S: What went through your head?

E: Well, the first thing, "How am I gonna raise my five children?" You know, being alone with five boys 'twas hard. I put my first five through school. It wasn't easy. And anyway, my oldest one, he became a dentist, and I'm proud of him because of that. The other ones, they all finished high school, and I'm happy for my children. Your father was kind of mysterious, but he was a sweet kid.

S: How old were you when you moved to the United States?

E: I came here in 1982 when I was 43.

S: What made you come to New Orleans?

E: Well, I remarried. I met my husband, and he was working up here and wanted us to come. And then I wanted a better future for my five kids. So that's the reason why I came here, because of them. They were all born in Honduras except for Cregg.

S: What did Grandpa have to do so you and your sons could come to the U.S.?

E: My husband now, he used to work with the

Above: Susan's uncles Erick and Cregg, courtesy of the Watler family.

banana company when he was back home. He came 46 years ago in a small boat, looking for a better opportunity. When he wanted to bring me over, he had a good job and a good reputation, and they helped him. He put in for my papers to come up here and he sponsored my children. He didn't adopt them, no, but he sponsored them at the American consulate in Tegucigalpa. And he took them up as his step-children. From my first husband, the youngest was 12. I had two for him. The oldest one for him was five years old and the youngest one was born here.

S: Have you met a lot of Hondurans here?

E: A lot.

S: Are you for real? I was gonna say I don't know anybody.

E: I met a lot of Hondurans here, mhm.

S: Who? I want to know.

E: A lot of people that work with me.

S: Oh, you don't have no friends? No?

E: I have a few Honduran friends, not too many. My pastor's from Honduras also. From a little island named Utila. I go to the church in Avondale. Sundays and Wednesdays he preaches in English, and Saturday and Thursday in Spanish. I go on Sundays because we grew up speaking English back home.

S: How often did you go back to La Ceiba?

E: Since I moved to stay? Once a year.

S: Can you tell me some stories about meeting me when I lived in La Ceiba?

E: You liked to do your own washing, your own laundry. You got up in the morning before you went to school and made your own breakfast. One time we came to visit your mom. My husband liked to watch the news, you know.

S: All day, every day.

E: And so your mama said, "Stephanie, let yo grandpa see the news." You let him watch maybe about ten or 15 minutes and came back to him and said, "Chingos, chingos!" You wanted him to get off the T.V. to watch cartoons, yeah.

You were a little girl. You had it hard. I used to worry about you a lot over there because you were along with your mama. You had to take care of your little brother and that's the reason why I wanted your daddy to bring you up. [*Tears*] She was a bright girl, your mama. It was just after she had the last little boy that she started getting that way. I don't think it's depression. I think it's schizophrenia.

S: How do people here react when you tell them you're from Honduras?

E: I work at Walmart as a cashier and and some Spanish people say things that they shouldn't be saying in Spanish, and they don't know I understand every word they say.

S: Mhm, yeah. And we do.

E: Sometimes I answer them in Spanish and they're surprised, "Oh, you speak Spanish. I thought you were from here." And I say, "I'm not."

S: What has been hard about living in a different country?

E: It's really not hard, not living.

S: Yeah it is. You're always talking about going back to Honduras.

E: Yeah, it's hard because I love my country. I love my home and it's hard for me to go home and be with everybody and—

S: Come back.

E: I come back and all my sisters and brothers are there. I miss my friends, I miss my city.

The black Americans, they're so different than us black people from different countries. Where I work, they don't sit with me too much because they say I'm Spanish. I try to treat all them equal like I would like them to treat me. Sometimes it's been difficult working with them. I don't know why they're like that because all of us should be alike.

S: We're all black.

E: Just because I come from a different country.

S: I remember girls making jokes. They'll be like, "You can't come from another country and take our boys."

E: We speak differently, you know, and sometimes I might say something they don't understand. If you don't have the education like them, they look down at you.

S: What do you miss most about Honduras?

E: I miss the climate, the foods—rice and beans, stew chicken, stew meat, Honduran cakes. I miss my family, my friends. Back home, you're more relaxed. Life is hard because you're poor, but not because of the stress. You have to work hard, but besides that it's nice. People in the United States, if they don't work, they still eat. Back home, the government won't give you a house and give you food.

Susan Henry interviews her grandmother, Elenor Watler, by Rachel Breunlin.

Interview with My Grandpa, Andres Watler

Andres Watler and Susan, by Abram Himelstein.

I love my grandpa. My grandma and him are always fussing at each other. In the car, it's all about directions or the way he drives. Once Grams started to work at Walmart, he missed her cooking and so she showed him how to cook some of his favorite food. He loves plantains and grilled fish. He's pretty good.

He works all day outside, cutting the grass. Sometimes it sounds like he's building things out there, but when I go outside, there's nothing there. He loves gambling, too.

Twenty-five percent of the words in his sentences include shit, especially when he's mad. My uncle Cregg and I tease him. I'll be like, "Man, stop leaving all this dishes in this sink, man." And my uncle Cregg will add, "shit."

My grandpa and I never talked about his past. I knew he was a seaman, but I didn't know where he went, or where he would go when he left for months at a time. I knew the reason we could live in the States was because my grandmother was married to him, but I didn't know why we could have papers and others, like my friend Pamela's family, couldn't. This interview was a good chance to talk about it.

Susan: Where did you grow up?

Andres: I was born in La Ceiba and raised up on Roatán. Some of my mother's people were from Roatán and some were from Barrio La Barra on the Mosquito Coast. They call it "La Barra" because it's close to where the Patuca River empties into the Caribbean. You got Garifuna there, you got the Spanish ones, and then they also got a couple of Mosquitos around there—a few. There used to be more. Besides bananas, the Mosquito Coast is known for Mahogany. My father was a carpenter and made tables, chairs, and beds out of the wood.

S: What is the banana trade like in La Ceiba now?

A: The Standard Fruit Company was based in a La Ceiba. The dock was in the ocean. The water gets too rough, especially in the wintertime, and the ships can't sometimes go around. They shut down the port and moved it to Puerto Castilla—a bay. They ship banana in containers now instead of in boxes. The 40-footers, 20-footers, 45-footers. But La Ceiba just keeps going up. They have hotels all over the place now.

S: Why did you want to move to New Orleans?

A: I came from Honduras on a fishing boat and got off in Miami. I was not an employee on the fishing boat, but I wanted to come up to the States to look for a job. I wound up on a little bigger ship than the fishing boat and stayed on for three months. Then, I got on a passing ship where I had an American visa, which allowed me to be on the foreign ship, or be ashore until the visa ran out.

I chose to get my residency and after I got my residency, I got off the foreign flag ship. I stayed ashore in New York for about two years. Then I got tired because there was no future working ashore—for me, anyway. I decided to join a Merchant Marine, and from there I started working with the Maritime Union (NMU) and went overseas. When I retired, I had about 35 years with the union. I've been all over the world almost. I haven't been to the Baltic Sea —that's about the only place I haven't been.

I lived in New York for 17 years and then I moved back and forth from Honduras for eight years. I retired from merchant seaman back in 2004— after I got sick and I couldn't go back to work. Otherwise, I'd probably still be working. When my family was coming up here, I moved to New Orleans because it's better place for them than New York. To me, New Orleans is almost like La Ceiba. You know, these old big houses, remind me of parts of Honduras. That's the reason why.

S: How did you meet Grandma?

A: I had known her from the time she was a young girl. Me and her husband were kind of friends. I found out that he had passed away. I was just getting my divorce and I was not ready to get in love. But because I knew her, I said, "Well, I'll take a chance." If I didn't know her, I would've never married her.

S: What did you have to do so that grandma and her sons could come to the U.S.?

A: Well, I had to fill out a lot of papers, a lot of documents. We took them to Immigration and that's the way I got her to come up here—her and the kids.

S: How would you describe the Seventh Ward for people who don't know?

A: Some of the other places we lived were too cluttered. It's much better environment here.

S: What would you like for me to know about the place where I come from? Honduras.

A: I don't know what to say about that. [*Laughter*] Everybody chooses their own life. Some people come up here and love it so much, they don't want to go back to Honduras. And some want to go back.

S: Have you met a lot of Hondurans here?

A: Oh, all kinds of Hondurans in this place. This place is like being in Miami with the Cubans.

Susan's house on Bruxelles, by Susan Henry.

Bruxelles

I always wanted my own home. Three years after we moved to the states, we found a home on Bruxelles Street, right off North Broad. I had my own privacy, that's all I wanted, to be alone. I would write, draw, read, sew clothes, listen to music, and even talk on the phone with no one to disturb me.

There was a beauty salon next to my house in Bruxelles. I dreamed of working there when I turned 16. I would sit on my little spot and just stare at the sign.

Interview with My Dad, Part II

Alston Henry, by Susan Henry.

When I was little, I saw my dad as my hero. It was a relief when he was home. He was so patient with my mom and she'd calm down when he was home, but she'd still do things. I wanted him to be around because then I didn't have to be in charge. If she did anything, he would take care of it. One time he cooked red beans and rice and she put spoonfuls of sugar in it. Another time, she put frozen pancakes in the microwave and used them to make herself a nasty sandwich with mustard, ketchup, and leftover chicken.

My family is very private, but sometimes my mom's illness made us call for help. One time she threatened me with a knife and I called my dad crying. He told me, "Call the police and I'll be there as soon as I can." When he got back to our house, she told him nothing's wrong. He said, "Put that knife down."

When my mom wasn't sick, he left everything up to her and she took care of us. I don't know what their relationship was like as a couple, but we didn't spend that much time together as a family. I was so focused on her sickness that I didn't think about how my parents felt about raising us in a new country. The problems in our home were so big that I put La Ceiba out of my mind. I wanted to interview my dad to get him to open up about what it was like to finally live with us. We didn't talk directly about my mom. He didn't want to talk about it.

49

Emmanuel and his cousins during Christmas, courtesy of the Henry family.

Susan: What is it like to raise children in New Orleans?

Alston: Anywhere you're at it's hard to raise children. It doesn't have to be here.

S: No, because I'll usually hear you say things like, "It's harder to raise children in the United States."

A: Well, in a way it's harder to raise you here because everybody is working, not just the husband. Over here, nobody has time for anybody.

In Honduras, your neighbors are closer. It's not that private. Here you might never know where your neighbors were born, where they're from. In La Ceiba, your parents tell you, "This is this man. I know his grandmother. I know his great-grandfather. But here, you have no one to tell you.

S: Maybe you go outside you see your neighbor but over here everybody has their door locked.

A: That's all you do here, watch T.V. Here we stay inside because I never know anybody and I can't trust anybody.

S: When did you start smoking cigarettes?

A: I was working in the French Quarter at the Pelican Club. One of my friends from Honduras was smoking a cigarette. I was so goddamn worried—my wife was over there, my kids were over there—and I wanted to go home. I asked my friend why he felt like smoking that cigarette. He said if I smoked, I'd know. He gave me one of them and I started smoking. If I have a couple drinks, I smoke my cigarette.

S: I thought you stopped.

50

A: No, I had only stopped for a month or two.

S: When did you start drinking?

A: The first drink I had was when I was 10 years old.

S: How did you start?

A: I was staying in Barrio de la Julia. One Christmas, one of your uncles, Lydia's brother, brought some wine and I drank a whole bottle that night. I didn't know what the hell it was, but I drank it.

S: What was one of your goals as a child? What did you want to do when you grew up?

A: I'm the kind of person that I never had something special in my mind. Whatever got in front of me, I would try to do it because it's nice to have something. That's the kind of way I feel.

S: Do you think your childhood has much to do with the way you interact with your family?

A: What you mean?

S: Like for Christmas sometimes you would just be in your own little world. Sometimes it would feel like you wouldn't want to be like too close with the family.

A: Sometimes I enjoyed being alone the most. I've been like that since I was small. Being happy is the way you want to be—that's what I think about life. Making somebody else happy, and you're not happy, why do it?

S: How did you learn how to cook?

A: By watching my mother. I just do what I feel like doing. I cook anything—fried plantain, *baleadas*, tortillas, refried beans, and cheese.

S: I always eat what you cook.

A: Everybody else fries the beans. I fry them, but first of all, I put them in the blender with jalapeno peppers, onions, and seasonings. I blend it and *then* I fry it.

S: You make some good red beans. I would never eat them but when you would make them they would be different. How long did you play soccer?

A: Man, I've played soccer since I was seven years. I started playing in Barrio La Isla. Our yard was big and we used to invite over friends to play. After my daddy died, we bought a house in Englishtown, where the Standard Fruit Company used to be. The dock and train tracks used to be over there, and they used to be getting all those bananas and packing them into the ships. We were divided from the Standard Fruit Company by a fence. On the other side is where all the workers lived. The fence had a big hole, and everybody from our town used to sneak through it and go play soccer. I played in college at the Instituto San Isidro as well. I stopped playing soccer when I was 39.

S: Why did you stop?

A: Because I hurt my knee. I played middle, I played front. I played anywhere I could have played.

S: I think that's the most we have interacted with Spanish people and Honduran people because every Saturday we would go to the soccer field in City Park to watch you play. Would you go back and live in Honduras?

A: Of course, yes. That's my country. I don't want to die here.

S: I thought you were gonna be like, "Because I like it over there because of the trees, because of the food."

A: Yeah, because of the trees, the ocean. I stay half a block from the beach.

S: Yeah, I talked about that in my book.

A: I just go out on the front porch and looked at the ocean—looked at the beach. If you wanted to do something you just walk. You want to go fishing?

Hey, you just do it. It feels so free. Everybody thinks this country is free. This country's not free. Whatever you do here, you gotta pay for it. In Honduras, you can plant your coconuts, mangoes, and sugarcanes behind your house. You don't need insurance for nothing.

This never will be my home. This last year was my longest time being here—I think 14 months—and it was the worst. All my friends are over there. Most of the time, you meet friends in school. You came here when you were small and have gone to school. I don't have roots here like you do. I know you can't be here with your mind and soul somewhere else.

What's Yo Name?

When I first saw Red, and some of the other boys from around Bruxelles, they were hanging out at McDonald's on Broad Street. From that day on, I couldn't keep my eyes off of him. He would go to school everyday looking so fresh and clean with a nice haircut. He even had a book bag. I always made plans to talk to him, but I never did until the day he made it happen.

I was walking home from school and passed his house.

"Say," he said.

I looked back to see if anyone was behind me. Then I asked him if he was talking to me, just to make sure.

""What's yo name?" he kept going.

"Stephanie," I answered. Even though it's my middle name, I always answer to that when I am not in school.

"How old you is?" he finished.

"I'm 13," I answered. I was so shocked and excited that I didn't even want to talk to him anymore. I just wanted to go home and jump up and down like crazy.

One day I was playing around with the little kids from the neighborhood and wrote Red a note saying that I didn't really like him and that it was all a joke. He came by me to ask me about it. I was sitting on the stairs of my front porch and he was dribbling his basketball. As he got closer, my heart started beating faster. He sat across from my little chill spot and said that he didn't understand the meaning of the letter. I told him I didn't write it.

We got into this long conversation and he popped the question, "So do you like me?" And I said, "Yes,"

And he said, "I like you, too." He told me the story

Susan in middle school, courtesy of the Henry family.

about his sister and how she gave him the scar on his face. As he got closer, and sat down next to me, I grew a little shy.

I knew his schedule. When he came home from school, he took off his uniform and would come back outside to play basketball or ride around on his bike. He had a dog he loved so much. I used to go outside and watch them play. His best friend was Gee. They were always together. They even had sleepovers. I would make fun of them for that. Sometimes Red woke up around eleven a.m. and walked down the street to Gee's house wearing just his pajamas and his socks.

Saturday used to be a party time at my house. Red and Gee came over and ate up all the snacks because we did groceries on Fridays. I had to keep my eye on Gee otherwise he'd have us making groceries the next day.

Sewing Machine

Susan with her sewing machine, by Abram Himelstein.

I asked my mother for a sewing machine but she insisted that I would get it, use it a couple of times, and leave it alone. She never understood how passionate I was about it. I wished so much for a sewing machine. When I made 13, I bought one from Walgreen's. It was a little one and only cost 40 dollars. It only lasted me three days. I brought it back after it stopped on me.

I got the money back and started saving up money from my allowances and doing chores for my uncles Erik and Cregg. I wanted one that I could use to make pillow cases, curtains, and chair covers for my grams. When I gathered a 100 dollars, I couldn't wait any longer and went to Walmart. The cheapest one was 78 dollars but the sky blue and white one that I wanted was 178 dollars.

When I got home, I was so disappointed. I told my mom and she said, "Take some money out of my purse and bring back the change." I went back to Walmart and got it.

Oh my God, I was so excited. When I got home, I grabbed all my clothes I couldn't fit and adjusted them to fit my small waist.

When I went to my grams' job, I'd go to Walmart's fabric section to look for fabrics and fashion magazines. I'd flip through them for ideas and then go home and sketch my own designs. I sew them when I find nice fabric to work with. I have my own personal photographer at home, too—my little brother. Sometimes he's in the mood and sometimes I have to beg.

Evacuation

I had just started my eighth grade year when the Hurricane hit. I remember the day as if it was yesterday. My dad was watching the news eight days before the storm. The day before the storm hit, my dad said we were leaving. I was shocked.

I went outside that night and sat on the stairs. I thought about all the things that could happen. I looked down the street and saw Red, Brenden, Rishad. I would not be able to sit on the stairs and watch them play basketball. I used to watch them play "hide-and-seek" at night. I wanted to play but was too scared to ask. Plus I would have been the only girl.

The night we left New Orleans, the only thing that was on my mind was saying goodbye to Red. The next morning, my dad woke us up and told us to pack our bags. Almost everyone on my dad's side of the family met at my grams' house. As the car pulled over I looked back and saw Red's mother's car sitting in front of the house.

We all drove to Atlanta to stay with my uncles' wife's parents. When we realized we wouldn't be coming back to the city right away, my grams wanted to go by her son in San Antonio so we got in the cars again and drove to Texas.

My parents didn't tell me what me what was going on. We stayed in a hotel and I was having a blast with my cousins. After a few days, my cousins said the adults decided that we would all go to Houston, where Katrina evacuees were getting help.

My dad decided to send us to La Ceiba while he set up our house in Houston. On our way to Honduras, we came back to New Orleans. The roof of our house had been torn off in the storm and a tree fell on the porch. Parts of the ceiling collapsed in my room and everything was wet and moldy.

After I looked at my house I walked down the block and noticed the mark on Red's house. I got scared because I had heard on the news that a mark meant that a dead body was found in the house. I wrote him a letter and dropped it at his door. It would be months until I saw him again.

Julio Popper map, courtesy of The Latin American Library, Tulane University.

Part III: Returns

Back to La Ceiba

The plane was big, but not as big as the one we got on when we first came here. I was excited, nervous, and scared. We flew into Tegucigalpa, the capital of Honduras, and had to stay overnight. My mom found us an ugly motel close to the bus station. It looked like a place where people rented rooms by the hour rather than the night. When my mom left us for a few minutes, I was counting the seconds until she came back.

The morning felt like it would never come. During the bus ride across Honduras, I saw people riding on horses, mama carrying their babies in slings on their back. When we stopped, people came on the bus to sell *pasteles* (meat pies), fried plantains, fresh orange juice and lemonade.

In La Ceiba everything seemed the same to me. We ran into someone my mama knew and he gave us a lift to my grandmother's house in La Julia. We hadn't seen each other in three years. I hugged her and she called me her *reina* like she always does.

We stayed for three months. I wasn't the same little girl that I was when I left. When I watched my grandmother's store, boys used to come to buy stuff just to mess with me.

Susan's grandmother Barbara on the beach in La Ceiba, courtesy of the Henry family.

I hung out with my cousins at soccer games and they invited me to parties where everyone would dance to hip hop, R&B, reggaetón, and bachata. I was asked to dance a few times, but was too shy. Towards the end of one night, I made a little circle with some of the girls and danced. Sometimes I'd hear my cousin's Spanish R&B band on the radio. I was proud that he was talented.

I started worrying about school. I didn't want to have to repeat again and missed my dad. My mother started getting sick again. She was jealous that her sisters were so close to her mom. She got upset and acted like everyone was against her. She'd call my dad at the Internet rooms and he'd reassure her, "It's okay, you'll be home soon."

Passport

My mom couldn't believe that her passport was expired. I couldn't believe it either. We stood at the counter as the lady behind it explained that she couldn't get on the plane. My brother and I had until 2010, but she only had until 2006.

My mom said that my brother and I would leave and she would stay to fix her situation. I won't lie— I was happy that she let us go, but I didn't want to leave her. I cried when we said goodbye and then started worrying, "How will I eat? She has all the money." She had to pay extra money for us because we were under age. Those were a lot of *lempiras*. The flight attendant gave us a little necklace with a plastic patch so we wouldn't lose our plane tickets. She showed us to our seat, and we sat down. My brother was crying, saying he wanted to stay, and I said, "No, don't be stupid, we're going back home. She'll come later."

We made a stop at Miami and waited in a room all by ourselves for a long time. It was full of light colors. I'm guessing it was meant for children. We tried to figure out how to get some snacks. I had some American change in my purse, but they were mostly pennies. We had enough for a honey bun.

We landed in Houston with the black night and bright colors on the ground. We called my dad and waited for him at the baggage claim. The airport was getting ready to close and he was still taking a long time. When I saw him, he was wearing a black cap,

Emmanuel at the Henry's apartment in Houston, courtesy of the Henry family.

a black polo shirt (that's all he wears) and some jeans with some black tennis shoes. He helped us with our bags and we walked to the car, talking about our trip and asking what took so long. He said, "Houston is so big, I kept getting lost on the highway."

"We're hungry, did you cook? Mama had to stay."

"Yeah, she told me. All she needs to do is renew her passport"

I couldn't wait to see my new apartment. I was shocked. It was beautiful. Everything looked so new— fresh paint, carpet. My brother and I shared a room, but hey, we had our own walk in closets big enough for all my heels and belts. We still didn't have furniture but about a week later we got new beds, dressers, and some other basics. We even had a balcony and a pool. I knew my mom would be so happy when she saw it herself.

When she came back, she was so glad to see us that she was like her old self. She helped figure out how we'd get into school again and I started to think maybe we could start our lives over again in Houston.

59

Susan's school in Houston, courtesy of the Henry family.

School in Houston

I went to Jane Long Middle School across the street from our apartment. The girls hung in the restrooms just to put on their eyeliner and talk about boys and the next party. The kids thought that I was like the other New Orleans girls until they got to know me. There were a lot of immigrants from Mexico and from all over Latin America, although no Hondurans. Many of them didn't have any papers, but they made it through and lived well in Houston. They spoke Spanish and were surprised to hear a black girl talk back.

I had one friend who was from Mexico and didn't speak any English. When we were in small groups together, she asked me to translate. Our apartment complex had a pool and she came over to swim one time with her sister. The complex was so big, we jumped into each of the three pools. My little brother always liked when I brought people over because he didn't have many friends. He usually doesn't like speaking Spanish because he was so young when he moved to the States, but we all talked in Spanish that afternoon. My brother with his New Orleans Spanish accent, me with my La Ceiba Spanish, and our friends with their Spanish from Mexico.

Not Again

My dad was working in New Orleans, helping to rebuild the Superdome and getting good money for it. He drove to Houston on Fridays, and came back to work in New Orleans on Sundays. I had to go to summer school because I started school too late. My mom told me that my dad was thinking about bringing us back to New Orleans. I explained to my dad that I had to go to summer school because I started the year too late. I was crying because I didn't want to fail, but he said I could go to school in New Orleans. I said, "I don't want to have to repeat," I'd already done that one time because of our move to the States.

I'm decided, "Man, I'm not listening to him. I'm not going to listen to him. If he makes me leave, I'm gonna report him to the police." I was so serious, I went the first day. They had us seated and were separating them into two groups. The teacher was saying, "These are the students that have to continue coming to summer school. And these are the students that only need to be here today because you were good students during the year and your teachers don't have any complaints about you." I was on that list.

I walked home crying. I didn't care where they took me—I just knew I didn't have to go back to eighth grade.

Everybody was packed except for me. My mom said, "Get the necessary things." I thought we were staying for just a little while. I picked up two pairs of heels, tennis shoes, flip flops, church clothes and jeans. Enough for a couple of days.

After being back at my gram's house for a while, I started feeling like the visit was getting a little long. I said, "When are we going back?" My mom said, "We aren't."

"What? I finally got a computer and we have to leave it?? I mean, are we going to go back to pick up our stuff?"

"It's all up to your dad."

But my dad always says, 'What's the point of having lots of stuff when I can't bring it with me when I die."

61

Too Small

The new apartment, by Susan Henry.

At my gram's, we shared a one bedroom with two beds. I thought we'd never get out of her house. It was hard to look at my cousins and their lifestyle while we had left everything behind three times—once in La Ceiba, once when we evacuated for Katrina, and now a third because we weren't going back to Houston. My dad had been living in the U.S. for the same amount of time as his brothers and they all had their own homes and nice jobs in the suburbs on the Westbank or in Metarie. They all wanted to make their own way without my grams. But my dad wanted to be close.

In 2007, we rushed out of Grams' house and moved to a two-bedroom apartment at the back of a small corner store. It was obvious we had overstayed our welcome. I didn't want to move in. I didn't like it. For 1,100 dollars a month, it seemed too small. The roof leaked and the kitchen and den were just one room. I never planned to have sleep overs in there, nor friends over. To me, it was embarrassing. I asked my grams if I could stay with her and she said, "No, I didn't think they'll let you stay. They need you around with them."

Emmanuel and I were supposed to share a room, but I kicked him out and claimed it as my own. He slept with my parents or on the couch. He'd tell me, "You're wrong for kicking me out. This is my room, too." But I wanted privacy to write and to talk on the phone late into the night. He curled up on the couch and left the lights and T.V. on. Sometimes I missed him, and we'd make popcorn and watch movies in bed.

Red

I enrolled at John McDonogh Senior High and ran into Red again. We walked home together one day and talked about how things were back in the day. He told me his dog died after the hurricane. His grandmother took him to the vet. She didn't want to see it suffer because it was old and very sick. They gave him a shot and killed him.

He lost touch with Gee after he moved Uptown. I guess Uptown had beef with Downtown or something like that. When I asked Red about Gee he told me he saw him once but Gee didn't speak so he didn't either. I used to see Gee in school and he never talked to me except for once when he asked me for some candy. I don't know why they stopped being friends, but whatever the reason, I think it was stupid.

He asked me what was I going to do on Sunday.
"Nothing."
"Do you want to go to church with me?"
"Yes."
"I'll pick you up in the morning at ten."

I woke up early to fix my hair. At ten I was outside waiting. I had on my favorite sky blue shirt with matching blue heels. Ten-thirty came and he still wasn't there.

When I called, he didn't answer the phone. At 12:20 I finally hear my phone ring. It was him saying, "I woke up late. I'm so sorry."

I forgot I was mad.

During my sophomore year, Gee was shot and killed outside a club. I used to always see happiness in Red's eyes, but now he seems tired and depressed, as if he's giving up or something. I see him fuss with teachers and sometimes cut class. He is so good at basketball that I thought he would play for John Mac, but no—he said he played for his old school and so he has to sit out for a year.

My First Boyfriend

I started getting noticed. I walked down the hallway at school and boys told me things they thought I wanted to hear—sexy, slim, beautiful. Someone called me "Pretty Eyes" when I wore hazel contacts and let's not forget "Red," because of my skin complexion. Despite the compliments, I looked in the mirror everyday, and I still didn't see what they see. I remember elementary school and know how it could be again.

My family is crazy. They feel that all boys are bums and players and, at my age, I can't find someone decent. I'll admit it's almost true. No teenage boy is ready to settle down. One of my uncles said I can't get married until I'm like 45 and I can't date until I'm 38. I'm guessing he's not serious. My grandmother said I can't have a boyfriend until I get out of college and I know she means it.

My uncle Cregg is like my guide into what boys do and how they get all the girls. Everything I heard in the streets I've heard him say to other girls. I tell him everything about boys and he's there listening and laughing at me. He warns me after I described them to him. My sophomore year, I met a boy who I really liked. His name was Johnboy.

1.

My uncle Cregg warned me, "That lil rich nigga gone just want to have fun with you cause he got money."

2.

When we started off, it was so sweet and innocent. I was the quietest girl in school and everybody made him the popular pretty boy. I was an outcast and I loved it. They said I was like a witch with my black hair and black fingernails.

3.

A mutual friend acted as messenger between us and passed on his number.

4.

I couldn't wait anymore. I called him. The phone rang once. "I shoulda never called," I thought.
It rang twice.
"Hang up."
I kept going.
It rang the third time.
"He's not going to answer."
He did.

"Waz up?"
He knew it was me.

5.

We sat in front of the T.V. at his house by the bayou. It was my first kiss. I felt overwhelmed and said, "It's late and I have to go home now."

6.

We talked every night that week. He brought me home from volleyball practice and I asked, "So are we gonna make this official?"

7.

He was my first boyfriend. It lasted a few days. He wanted us to get more physical. I said, "Can't we just not do it?" I didn't want to break up, but we were at an impasse.

8.

We communicated and got mad at each other like we were still together.

JB: You don't have to call or text if it's a problem.

Me: Why you say that?

JB: Because you be trippin for nothing. You play around too much.

Me: You know I be wanting to talk to you, but when I call you be like, "I'ma call you back."

JB: Whatever. I'm not going to worry about you. Don't Call.

Me: You'll always have a special place in my heart, my one and only lil Devil. In the future we might cross each other. You a famous football player, me a fashion designer and start all over.

9.

At lunch, I saw him at that table with all those girls. I didn't care because I was on the phone. He looked at me and I looked at him. He said, "Which one of y'all want to be my next girlfriend?"

"Don't you have a girlfriend?" one asked.

"I broke up with her."

He came by and asked me why I didn't want to talk to him anymore.

"You're the one who's acting funny."

He kept staring at me, but I played it off. I looked up and saw a passion mark on his neck and put my head down again.

10.

I was still thinking hard and woke up with bags under my eyes. I took my red lipstick and gave myself three passion marks. They looked real. I put my uniform on. No belt. My shirt untucked. My hair in an uneven pony tale. No lip gloss. No earrings. After my fourth period class, I walked out of the classroom stretching, "after a long night."

11.

I went on his MySpace. His status was single but I saw a picture of a white girl with long black hair, almond shaped eyes, and a pretty smile. He told me that was his friend, but I had the feeling it was more than that.

12.

Sometimes he still calls me, but I can't go back to being that shy girl.

Interview with My Uncle Henry, Part II

After Katrina, my uncle Henry came back after staying in New York for awhile to be closer to his son. Since he's been back in New Orleans, he's been working in a shop, and helping out my mom a lot. I love going to see him. The smell of hair spray and products instantly shocks my smell senses. It's filled with lights with mirrors everywhere—big and small. Pictures are framed on the wall with beautiful women and the T.V. is always on. There are glass stands with brand new hair products to be promoted. A desk at the door with papers, pencils, a Bible, and a laptop. No one sits behind it. When people come up to it to get seated, my uncle's girlfriend usually just calls out, "How may I help you?"

Being in any shop brings me back to when I used to watch my mom. Sometimes when my uncle's girlfriend asks me if I would like to do someone's hair, I worry I won't do a good job, but the clients always seem happy.

It's an environment I look forward to being a part of. Waking up Wednesday through Saturdays to open a shop. Conversations with people and making them feel good about themselves while getting paid to do something that I love.

I wanted to ask my uncle about his journey to New Orleans from Honduras. Hearing his story was sad. We're pretty close anyway but this interview made it obvious to me how much we look to each other for support and inspiration.

Henry Brooks, by Susan Henry.

Susan: What do you think were your biggest mistakes as a teenager?

Henry: It was being a gang member. I regret it because in a small town without rules. We don't have cops, it's basically corrupt. If you don't agree with the gang members, they're gonna kill you. They have control over the whole neighborhood.

I got into the gang because I happened upon a conversation and heard too much. They threatened me. If I didn't join, they would kill me or someone in my family. The gangs could find you anywhere in Honduras. It's something like the mafia. I started getting really scared. I'm the type of guy who likes to work a lot and hear my mom say that she's proud of me. One of the gang members told me that we were supposed to go rob a store, and I didn't want to do it. Then I went to Roatán trying to hide from the gang members.

They called me and told me if I didn't show up, they were going to hurt one of my brothers, so I decided to show up again. They were asking me to make a tattoo of the name of the gang on my arm. My mom raised us in church, "If you make a tattoo on your body, God doesn't think that's right."

I left Honduras for three reasons. For a better life, because I could lose my life, and for my family. I decided to come to this country.

S: How old were you when you came to New York?

H: Oh man, that's a good question.

S: I know you were young.

H: I was young. Okay, picture me in New York—a country boy in the middle of the big city. He doesn't know anybody. He doesn't know nowhere to go.

S: You didn't say how old you were.

H: Oh, by that time I was like 20.

S: And you said you came here because of the gang?

H: Yeah, running from the gang members because they were gonna kill me—basically trying to save my life. I went to New Jersey because my aunt was there. I got up early in the morning every day, trying to get a job. Everything started getting really, really hard. I was passing by a barbershop and I see this Dominican dude in there. I asked him for a job and he asked me if I got my papers ready. I told him, "Yeah, I got everything, man. About the only thing that I don't got, I don't got no clippers." He said, "Don't worry about it. You come try out tomorrow. You're gonna start working."

When we finished working that week, I was making 50 dollars a week, sending out money to Honduras. I decided to move to New York, because everybody used to tell me New York is the city where nobody sleeps. I thought I could make some money. I started looking for a job in Manhattan. I was walking and walking and walking. Then, when I realized I wanted to go back to New Jersey, I don't know how to do it. Damn, I started getting scared. It was freezing. I called my aunt, "Please come and pick me up."

Well, she wouldn't pick me up. I found one of my boys from back home. He was living in Brooklyn and I started explaining to him my condition.

He said, "You're my brother. You could come to my

house." I said, "Man, you sure?" I stayed a weekend and he found me a job.

S: You worked in a small shop selling fruit.

H: Not selling the fruit, but helping the people put the boxes on the truck. And they used to tip me. I was starting to get good money. When I'm saying good money, like 30 dollars a day—everybody helping everybody. I said, "Damn, this is better than working in the shop." Then I found my baby mama.

S: You don't have to answer that now, because I got questions for you.

H: Oh, all right. I'm sorry.

S: In the beginning, when you got to New York, how was it different from Honduras?

H: It was really crazy, man. I used to feel that everything was so crowded. It was blowing my mind. I was getting sick. I started freaking out, but then I started getting used to it.

S: Why did you move to New Orleans? To come and see us, right?

H: When I was living in New York, I got involved with a lady over there—with my baby mom. Her roots are in Honduras, but she grew up in the city. We were dating almost for one year, and moved in together. Everything was going good. By that time I was working in a welding shop. I was getting 500 dollars a week. I was ready to start a family.

I used to be so busy working that I wasn't paying attention to her. She told me almost every weekend,

"Let's go out. Go to the movies." I was like, "No, I need to work because I need to take care of my family back home." We were together five years, and if you ask me if I took my baby mama to the movies at least one time, I'm gonna be lying to you if I say yes. She got sick of that and started seeing someone else. I remembered my sister was over here, so I came to New Orleans.

S: What was it like when you moved over here?

H: I wasn't liking it because I was already adapted to the running around over there in New York. This city was kind of country. But I started talking to myself. I said, "But you're coming from the country, Henry, so what are you talking about?" Everything was slow, slow, slow for me.

S: How did the relationship with the family change after moving over here?

H: I was looking to be close to my family because over there in New York I was by myself. Sometimes it doesn't matter how big you look, how strong you look, sometimes you need your family around you. I decided to stay over here to be close to my sister, because she was in a bad situation at the time, too.

S: How did you deal with being black and from Honduras in the States?

H: For me, being black over here and being Hispanic is like, "Wow." Every time I open my mouth, I get a lot of attention. People don't believe me. They think that I'm African American, and I'll tell them straight up I'm Spanish. I can't even read English. I went to Spanish schools.

S: Would you rather be here in New Orleans or in New York and why?

H: I would like to be in New York for my son, but I also want to be close to my family. I learn a lot over here in New Orleans.

S: Would you go back to Honduras?

H: I would love to, but not to live anymore.

S: Just to visit?

H: Yeah, because I can't provide for my other family members if I'm over there. I could do it from over here, but not over there because the money is too low over there.

S: People would probably stop coming over here if there was more money.

H: Yeah, I'd take all of my family and go back home.

S: Did you always want to go to school and actually make a career out of barbering?

H: Hell yeah, not even the barbering. I would love to go to school and do a lot of stuff.

S: Well, my vision is for all of us to have our own shop. You're one of my closest uncles—the closest I always call you.

H: I don't even see you like my niece. I see you like my daughter.

S: What were your biggest dreams?

H: I mean, I just did it. I manage my own barbershop. Sometimes I see myself and I don't even believe it. I don't know how I did it, but I did it. My dream came true over here. The only thing is that the barbershop is not under my name. I want it under my own name.

You're not waiting for anybody. You already know that you've got to go and get it. A lot of the people over here think, "Daddy gonna give me a car when I graduate from school." You already know that you're not gonna have that. You got to work for it. That's one thing about being a Honduran. Keep doing what you're doing. You know you already got my support. I want to say that I'm really proud of you.

Susan and her uncle Henry, by Lindsey Darnell.

Registration for cosmetology licenses in Mrs. Richardson's classroom, by Susan Henry.

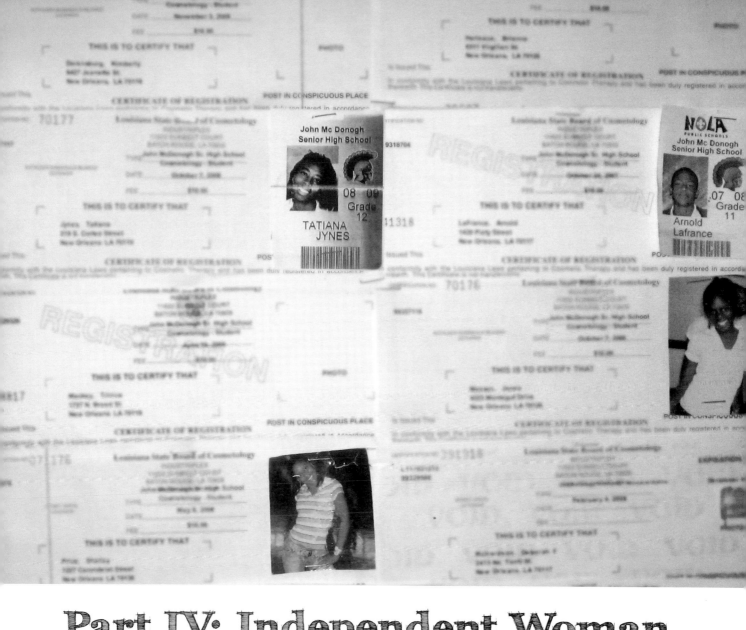

Part IV: Independent Woman

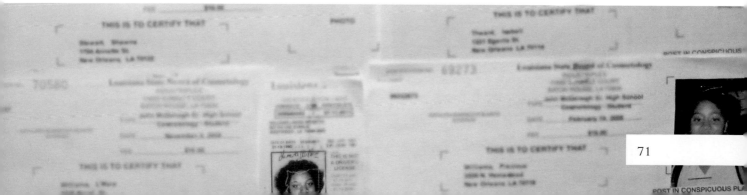

She's Gone

In 2007, my mom was acting crazy again. We were staying over at my grams' house while she and my grandpa were in Honduras. My uncle Cregg and I sat at the kitchen table playing around. My mom walked in, grabbed a frying pan off the stove, and threw it against the wall. Then she went to the glass table that weighs a ton, picked it up, and tossed it. We didn't know what to do. I wanted to pick up all the pieces because I had a vision of stabbing someone with one of the shards of glass.

One Friday afternoon, I was doing my cousin DeeDee's hair and my mom said she was going by a friend to do her hair. She didn't have anything with her—no combs, brushes or anything having to do with hair. I was worried and asked if my dad knew about it. She asked to see my phone to call him and left.

When my dad got home from work after midnight, she was still not home. Everyone was worried. I don't want to sound mean, but I kind of wasn't. I felt she knew what she was doing. The next day she was still gone. On Sunday, she called to tell me she was flying back to Honduras. She already had her ticket and it sounded like she was at the airport. She just wanted me to know she was okay.

I said, "Okay." I felt relieved that we knew where she was and tears rushed down my cheeks. I asked her, "Is this what you want to do? Is this what's going to make you better?" She said, "Yes, I have a plan. I'm going to go work in a salon in the Cayman Islands. I'll still help you with whatever your need. I'll send you money."

"No, you're gonna be over there, you're gonna need all the money you can get to help yourself."

She begged I wouldn't tell my dad about her plans. I couldn't believe my ears. I didn't know what to do. I walked out the front door and went for a walk—a long walk. I wanted to just walk and walk.

Interview with My Dad, Part III

Alston Henry, by Susan Henry.

My mom didn't go to the Cayman Islands. She stayed in La Julia with my grams Barbara. She was sick again. At this point I feel that the only way that I can help her is by helping myself and looking out for my brother.

My dad gave me a calling card to call my mom. I wasn't doing anything at the time. I could have called her then and there, but I didn't. The next morning he made a big deal about it and insisted that I was, or am, being unfair and mean. He told me, "After all I've been through with her, I'm still here. I know you went through a lot with her, too."

I used to think my dad caused the problem because he was gone a lot, but as I grew older, I started to see how hard it must have been for him. He told me, "You will have children someday and you will know what it's like when your children are not there for you."

He offered to take me to school because of the cold weather. I could tell he was trying to keep the conversation going, but I kept quiet. Then he started to talk again, "Your mother is over there suffering, wishing she was here with us. The least you could do is consider calling her."

I got out of the car and thought of how my mother treated my grandmother when she was younger. How she took her dad's side when my grandma was miserable. How, out of anger, my grandmother told my mom she would pay for all the things she did as a little girl. In my case, it's different. I didn't do anything. My mom's mental illness is what caused it all. I decided to talk more with my dad about how he feels about her being gone.

Susan: What was it like when you found out that mom was going through a mental illness?

Alston: At the beginning, I didn't know if she was sick because she was acting normal. But she used to accuse me for things I wasn't doing. I used to be thinking, "Why she was acting like that?" She wanted to make me be the bad guy.

S: I kind of explained in the book that it really didn't seem like to me as if it were depression because of the things she would do.

A: People hide their mental illness. She can tell people any doggone thing and they can blame me. I used to do my best and I never, never got credit for what I was doing. It's rough. I like to talk to everybody, make friends, but maybe because I was doing that a lot of people used to go tell her I was doing this, doing that.

S: Why do you think she left?

A: She left because she wanted to leave. Nobody forced her to do anything. I know I didn't do anything for her to leave.

S: Would you like for mom to come back?

A: Yeah, of course I would like her to come back. She's your mom, she's my wife. I love her—whatever she did.

S: What needs to happen for her to be able to come back?

A: Well, I'm doing whatever I've got do with immigration.

S: What is it like to deal with the immigration issues for us to stay in the U.S.?

A: Immigration is kind of hard. I am a permanent resident, but I can't spend more than six months in Honduras or I will lose my status. I have to become a dual citizen, in Honduras and the States, then her paperwork will come faster.

S: What do you stress about more these days?

A: In this country, it's money. If you ain't got money in this country, you ain't got nothing. You have to pay for everything.

S: How do you feel about me writing this book?

A: Well, I'm just proud of you because like I always thought about writing about us. I started to write a book to show people that life is not just about what you got. It's how you live life.

S: Remember I was talking about it? About how God put you in this world for a purpose and that you shouldn't live your life on material things.

A: Material stuff, yeah.

S: Starting today what could I do to be the perfect daughter to you?

A: Baby, you was always a perfect daughter—from the beginning.

Mrs. Richardson at her desk, courtesy of Deborah Richardson.

Interview with My Cosmetology Teacher at John McDonogh, Deborah Richardson

At school, I saw the girls wearing their all-white uniforms and had no idea why, but I wanted one. I found out they came from the cosmetology department tucked in the corner of the second floor. I didn't know that the program existed. I talked to my counselor, Ms. Bethquit, about enrolling in the program. She convinced me that the right thing to do was to focus on the classes needed to graduate and go to college. I should have explained to her how important it was to me, and signed up then. When I made up my mind, it was in the middle of the school year. Too late.

Mrs. Richardson was the head of the program. She's bossy. Students think she's mean because she's hard on them, but I think she's the coolest. For my 11th grade year, she signed me up and explained that since I started later, it was possible that I wouldn't have enough hours to get my cosmetology license, but said by working at a shop I would be able to earn more hours. My dreams were becoming true until she said, "I just need your birth certificate, your social security card, and for you to get these papers signed by your parents."

Every week she reminded me until I finally explained my situation. "I just need a couple of weeks, Mrs. Rich."

"Okay, but I need these documents in order to get you registered to get your license. Can you get something stating

you are waiting to get your papers so that I can prove it and they can get your hours registered?"

"I'm sure I can. I'll ask my dad."

For days, I asked my dad, and he had excuses:

"I'm looking into that."

"I can't do anything."

"I will ask when I talk to the lawyer."

"I'll go next week."

"Next week has not made it here yet."

Sometimes he said, "If it was meant for you, it will still happen. You can still get your license later."

"But I'll have to pay for it. Why not now that it's free? Why have to do this all over? Why work so hard now and have to do it all over again?"

At least I never gave up and Mrs. Rich saw that in me. She's been a big part of my life since I became one of her students. Sometimes we joke around and she tells me I just need to get an American husband. I wanted to interview her because I feel like I relate to her more and more as I get older. I was interested to know her own story of how she got involved with doing hair and how she started this department that has been such a good opportunity for people at my school.

75

Susan: Where were you born and raised?

Mrs. Richardson: I was born and raised in New Orleans, Louisiana.

S: Did you like it?

Mrs. R: Yeah, when you are born and raised in the place, you don't really know any other place. And yes, I do like it.

S: What neighborhood did you grow up in?

Mrs. R: In the Seventh Ward. You want me to say all that? You want me to elaborate?

S: Yeah, to make it longer.

Mrs. R: Okay. My mother was a Metoyer from Natchitoches, Louisiana. She was actually born in Cane River. She moved to the city with my grandmother, Edwina, and the rest of her family. I was born on Cleveland Avenue as an infant, but as a young girl, I was brought up in the St. Bernard Project. I was not ashamed of it. And at the time, I didn't realize that I was considered part of a lower class of people because of where I lived. There were a lot of neighbors and I enjoyed it. There wasn't a lot of crime. We did have dope fiends in the hall shooting dope, but they didn't bother us.

It was a very lively neighborhood—full of grocery stores. There was always somebody in the development selling frozen cups and candy. We walked everywhere because we didn't have transportation. The laundramat was about a mile away from the house and we had to go with pillowcases on our backs full of clothes.

S: What did you do for fun?

Mrs. R: We used to fly kites, jump rope, pick the flowers from the four-leaf clover and tie them together and make ropes. As a teenager, I started doing hair for my family. I started doing it as a hobby and people would give me little things—buy me a cookie. I would like to go to the grocery for people because they would let me keep the change and I knew that way I could always have some money.

We used to play jacks and this game called "pick in the dirt" where you used an ice pick and had to learn 12 different little skills. You had to go through all 12 skills without the pick falling out of the dirt. It had to stand straight up. I got really good at that. We used to shoot marbles. We used to play cards for money. We used to play "Ring around the rosy," "A tisket, a tasket." We used to play "Catch, kiss, get a little bit" and lots of other games we either made up or learned.

We would sneak off and walk to the bayou. We'd go to the park. We'd play "cool cans" and skate and jump on the back of somebody's car passing by and drag ourselves in the street. We'd play "pop the whip." We just played, played, played. And that's one of the reasons why I don't feel that I am as intelligent as I should be. You know, I should be smart. I should be a slight genius. I feel that way. If I would have applied myself in school, I know that I could have been a lot brighter than I am now. I try to instill that in my students and let them know, "Don't waste your time."

S: What did your mom do for a living?

Mrs. R: My mom is deceased. She died October the 8th, 2003.

S: So what did she do?

Mrs. R: She was a waitress and she worked at a very popular restaurant, Dooky Chase. She also worked at Chez Helene and Felix's in the French Quarter. Her last place of employment was at the Coffee Pot in the Quarter.

S: Did you ever go with her to the beauty salon?

Mrs. R: No, because she didn't go to the beauty salon that often. Only for special events because she had soft hair and it was straight. She really didn't have anything to do to it. She would get a haircut every now and then. If she was going to a ball, she would go to Maxie's—this guy who used to do hair that was in the neighborhood—and he would fix her hair in a big bouffant hairstyle. And then other times, when she just needed a hair cut, she would go to this other salon owned by Erlene Degruy, and I think it was Degruy's House of Style.

I don't know how I picked up doing hair. My mom worked at night. When we got up to go to school, she was not getting up to comb our hair. We'd be late every day waiting for her so I just started doing it myself in the first grade. It was a mess, but we had soft enough hair that we could just put it in a ponytail, put some oil on it, and it would be okay. We never took the tangles out.

On times when we would have special things at school, I wanted our hair to look nice so I would take a little extra time. When I started doing that, I learned how to part it straight and how to make new little ponytail styles. We'd use brown paper bags and twist them in our hair to make spiral curls because we didn't have rollers.

Deborah Richardson with her car in front of her uncle's store, courtesy of Deborah Richardson.

S: What were your major struggles as a teenager?

Mrs. R: My mom said we were moving out of the projects. I thought we were getting rich so I would tell my friends, "Oh, we're moving out of the project. We're leaving you in the project." And then the truck pulled up into another project. We left from the St. Bernard Project to the Lafitte Project. And it was basically the same type of environment.

I was not an average child. I started realizing as a teenager that I didn't want to live in the project all my life. When I would be at the bus stop and see young girls driving in cars and I would say, "Now she must have a mother and a daddy, because how could she afford to drive a car?" I said, "As soon as I am old enough, I am going to get a job and work to get me a car."

I had a lot of fear of going to my friends' houses and being around men by myself because I was always a target of somebody trying to molest me. Quite a few times I've had to fight somebody off me. It was difficult as a teenager and I couldn't understand it. I wouldn't discuss it with anybody, but it played on my mind and still does.

S: Did you ever get a relaxer?

Mrs. R: We used to get these liquid perms and comb it through our hair—it was called Tony Uncurly. And it would make our hair straight, straight, straight. But it wasn't a relaxer. After I got older, I started experimenting with relaxers and then I would get color. I wanted a permanent. It's not really a permanent, it's a relaxer, but everybody would say perm—"I need a perm." And one time I put a relaxer in my hair after I colored it and all my hair came out across the front, so I don't do relaxers anymore.

I wore it straight for awhile and then realized that it was high maintenance. I have curly hair and don't have to do anything to it. I let it grow out, cut it, and I have been wearing it short ever since.

S: How old were you?

Mrs. R: I must have been in tenth grade. Old enough to know that I was bald headed across the top for a while. I was introduced to the hair business when I started working after high school in the early '70s. I started working for my uncle Raymond, who owned Raymond's Barber and Beauty Supplies on the corner of Orleans Avenue and N. Tonti Street, right across from the Laffite Project. He was the first black person in the city of New Orleans to have as many employees as he did at one time.

I was a stock clerk. I started in a warehouse filling orders. Everybody would clown around, and I wouldn't clown because I didn't want to lose my job. I was finally getting a check. For three months, I didn't cash them. My uncle asked me, "You know, Deborah, we reconciled the bank statements and your checks are missing." And I said, "Well, I'm saving my checks to buy a car." And he said, "Baby, you can't save your checks." He said, "You have to get a bank account and cash your checks."

I was like a busybody there. Every time you filled an order, you had to put your initials in the book, and my uncle Raymond saw my name was always in the book. He would come in and say, "Well, why is this DF in the book 12 times and MW is in the book six times? She's doing twice that amount of work." He promoted me and let me work in the store where they sold beauty supply products. I was fascinated because they had so much there. I would read everything—all the labels—and if the beauticians came in to purchase products and asked me questions and I didn't know it, we would read it together and work it out.

I was able to go to a lot of hair shows and assist people that were well known in the business. My uncle Raymond would say, "You need to stay by her." This lady's name was Olive Benson. Jim Williams, Bill Madison, and all of these people were platform artists. I would be their gopher. They would talk to the beauticians that were at the show and say how much money they made. I just thought, "How could you make 1,000 dollars a day? He's not telling the truth." But after I started doing hair, I found out that it is very easy to make 1,000 dollars a day.

My uncle's wife had a beauty salon and when I would finish my work, I would sneak to the beauty salon and look through the crack in the door to see them work.

S: What was the significance of getting your hair straightened? Like you know, for people who get their hair straight?

Ms. R: Before the relaxer, they were doing a lot of pressing. When the relaxers became popular, it was so much easier with the climate and the weather that we have here. You would straighten your hair and then go outside and have it frizz up if it's raining, wasting a whole lot of time and money.

When the relaxers became popular, the companies would come and show us how to do it. It was just a much easier process than having your hair pressed and pulled with the straightening comb. And then the shop wasn't full of smoke from the oil. It was healthier.

S: Did you ever think you would be where you are right now, back when you were younger?

Mrs. R: No, I didn't know that I would be where I am now. In fact, I am almost ready to retire, but I knew that I was going to be something. I knew that I was going to eventually make money. I knew that I was not going to struggle all my life. It was a personal goal: I was going to either go to college or I was going to go to beauty school. Since none of my family graduated from college, I said, "Well, I'll go to beauty school later." As soon as I finished college, I went to beauty school. I graduated in December from Southern University in 1977 and I was enrolled in Stevenson Academy of Hair Design in January of 1978.

S: What do you do at John McDonogh?

Mrs. R: I teach cosmetology. I started the program in 1983 from the ground up—there was nothing

At school at Rabouin, courtesy of Deborah Richardson.

here. There was one at Rabouin. I was working there for a year-and-a-half, and then I was surplused —that means that they didn't need another teacher. I got word from the school board that the principal at John McDonogh was thinking about having the program and they asked me if I was interested in the job.

I got the job at Rabouin when I was working for my uncle after beauty school. When the manufacturers would come to demonstrate the products, I was included in a demonstration. They trained me how to do Lustra Silk curls. Lustra Silk was the same thing as Jheri Curls when that style was very popular. I would go to the salons and teach the hair stylists how to do it, and they would pay me. I went to Rabouin to do a demonstration for the students and the lady was so impressed. She said, "You just have a natural talent for this." The girls were making noise and she was an elderly little white lady—all nice—like a little Tinker Bell. And I was like, "You all have to be quiet. I can't explain anything to you when you are making all this noise." They sat down and they learned. They asked questions.

Mrs. Richardson in her early teaching years, courtesy of
Deborah Richardson.

After, she asked me if I was every interested in
doing teacher's training and I told her, "Yeah." But
that's the next level from being a cosmetologist and
I told her that I couldn't afford it because tuition
was 1,000 dollars. She said she would teach me and
I asked her when could I start. It was April and she
told me in the summer. During summer school, I
went to Rabouin and she taught me teacher's training in three months.

Before I went to take the test, I told her that there
was only one chapter I wasn't sure of and that was
eyebrow and lash tinting. She gave me a lesson. She
brought a customer in and we did a model. When I
went to state boards, you have to pull from a deck of
cards to find out what chapter you have to do a lesson
plan on. I pulled eyebrow and lash tinting and it was
a breeze for me.

I was still working in the store for Raymond's and
then he and his wife separated and the beauty salon
was closed for a long time. Business slowed and he
decided instead of laying me off, he would allow
me to manage the beauty salon. It was a six-station
salon—very big and exclusive.

S: What made you want to help others?

Mrs. R: Watching students learn and seeing how
eager they were to do hair and how some of them
had more talent than I did. It just inspired me to
want to help them. Once they started graduating and going into the profession, it gave me a little thrill. They own their own salons. Every time
I put another star up on the wall at the library—
you know, with my "Wall of Fame"—it just gives
you a good feeling to know that you were partially
responsible for these people's livelihood and for
making them productive citizens.

S: How old were you when you started working?

Mrs. R: 27.

S: What do you like about here?

Mrs. R: The kids are a lot like I was. You know, they
are from the same thread that I'm from. I've always
believed in passing it on. I make that reference to
them: "I used to be here. You can do this, you can do
this." Some of them get real close to taking the test,
start missing school, and freak out. I call their parents and let them know.

And right now, I don't figure that I am rich. I know
I'm not rich, but I'm rich in my feelings and my beliefs
that some of these kids just need a little bit of a push
and they can be successful. I know I'm successful and
I don't even want to be rich. I'm not struggling anymore. I love the song that John Legend, sings,

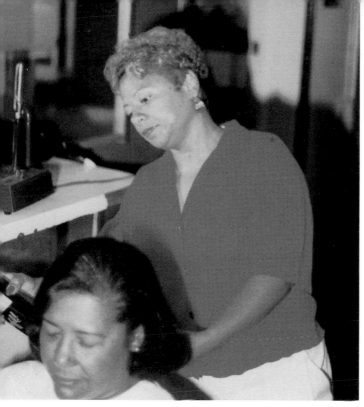

Teaching hairstyling, courtesy of Deborah Richardson.

We don't have to worry anymore.
No more putting it in the layaway.
You know, we finally got the money to pay.

S: Okay, what is something that you dislike about the school?

Mrs. R: What I dislike mostly about the whole situation of the high school is the fact that we change administrators a lot. We can have an administrator who is strongly in agreement with the program and then, the next year, we can get another administrator who is like, "Well, this is not important. We can eliminate this."

We are always in limbo. But we have been lucky. For the last 26 years, we have had about three administrators who have given us a hard time. For the most part, they agreed with the philosophy of the program and were proud that we had something to offer to the kids that was allowing them to leave right out of high school and become productive citizens.

S: What do you like mostly about being a hairdresser?

Mrs. R: Being a hairdresser or a teacher?

S: Well, a teacher.

Mrs. R: Okay, a teacher, hairdresser, teacher, we're mixing this up now. What I like most about being a hairdresser is that you can make somebody feel really good about themselves. You know, sometimes customers come into the school and they are not feeling really good about themselves and we look at them and we analyze their hair.

We analyze their complexion—we look at them and see what we can do to improve their look. And when they leave, they are smiling and feeling good about themselves. This field allows you to come in contact with people and you are almost like a psychologist because you have to convince them sometimes. They don't even want a haircut, but if you say, "Well, look at this. This is nothing but dead ends." And then when you cut their hair it's like, "Oh my gosh, I should have did this a long time ago." But convincing our people—you know, mostly a lot of African American people—to cut their hair is a major task. And when you do, it's a transformation.

A metamorphosis. All of a sudden, they care about their hair. They are here all the time. Even the students—when I cut their hair for them, you know, it's like, "Oh no, Ms. Richardson, don't cut my hair! Don't cut my hair!" But then they are in the mirror every day.

Now, they put tracks in and can have long hair today and short hair tomorrow. So I guess those ideas and philosophies may have changed with the times. In a couple of hours, you can transform an inch of hair to 20 inches of hair—like that!

S: When they find out that I'm not from here, they start saying like, "Are you white? Are you black?" Usually I wear the hair extensions and they would think that's my real hair. And they would be like, "Oh, her hair is good." Have you ever heard about having "good hair"?

Mrs. R: Well, ask me what is good hair.

S: What is good hair?

Mrs. R: Good hair is something that probably came from the Creoles or it came from a history with a lot of mixture of blacks. There are some blacks with fine curly hair and that would be considered "good hair" and if you have really tight curly hair, kinky hair that would be considered nappy hair or "bad hair."

Good hair, to me, is healthy—well-managed and well taken care of. If it's healthy, whether it's curly or kinky or straight, then the texture doesn't matter. When I hear "good hair" now from the kids, it bothers me because I know that's so cliché. It's so, so cynical.

But I was like that when I was younger. I was one of the ones that thought I had good hair. My hair was soft and I didn't need to get a relaxer and I could comb it easily, but it didn't make me a better person.

For a lot of families, hair has been a status thing because mostly bright people had good hair and they thought—and this is just generally speaking—they were a cut above, or an upper-class like the whites. We are all black, but because you're lighter than I am then you have a better chance at getting a job or getting accepted into other places than a darker-skinned person would have. That has not changed that much. And if you had "good hair," then you were in a different class.

But if you are light-skinned with nappy hair, then they'd call you, "Light-skinned, nappy haired ass." There are some dark-skinned people with hair like mine and it's almost like they don't fit in. It's like, "How do you get to have hair like this?" They are questioned about it because they figure that because you have brown skin, you should have the same kind of hair.

You know, usually when you have dark hair you have these "Negroid features," as they used to say. The first thing they would say, "Pickyhead-ass." They could call you a pickaninny in a minute and if you had a different kind of hair, it was just different. And if you had a different complexion, it was different.

You look at televisions shows and see the types of black people that get jobs. Most of those people have

Hair in training, by Susan Henry.

fine hair. Sometimes they'll say, "Well, we'll give you the job if you straighten your hair." You don't see a lot of nappy haired people on television. You know, you just don't, unless it's a movie about black people.

S: Have you already experienced someone judging you based on what kind of hair you have?

Mrs. R: Yes.

S: Yeah?

Mrs. R: Yes, they like me because I have good hair. Or they don't like this person because their hair is nappy.

S: What is the most popular kind of styles people use in New Orleans?

Mrs. R: They do a lot of the pin curl ponytails now. They like wear a lot of weaves. They wear a lot of short styles like mine—short and tapered. And they wear the spiky look. It's a variety. You get all kinds of styles in New Orleans. We put an emphasis on healthy hair—a lot of other places, people wear a lot of wigs.

The cosmetology program in action, by Susan Henry.

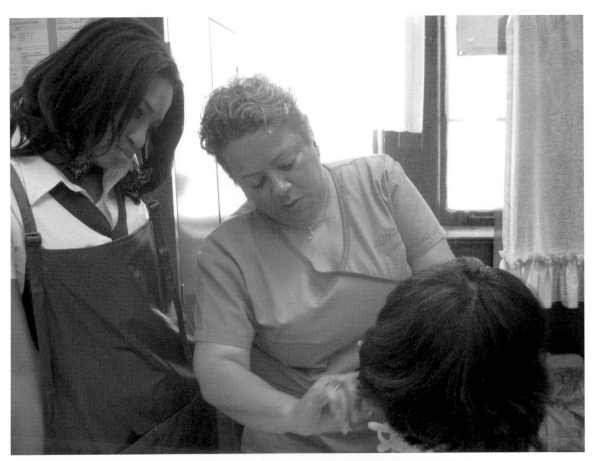

Left: Susan and Mrs. Richardson. *Right:* Susan and Marvin Payne. Photographs by Lindsey Darnell.

87

Different Methods

At church my pastor said,

God is love and if you don't love me, or have something against me, then you don't love God.

Sitting in the pew, the message caught my attention. I never had been so angry with someone the way I've been angry with my mother.

Since she's been gone, my dad's working with lawyers and spending money he doesn't have. He is putting her first. I guess she is now waiting on a letter from immigration. When she is able to come back, her papers will be straight and then ours—my brother's and mine.

I guess I can sacrifice for her to come back and be patient. I hope that this issue is dealt with before I graduate. I want to have everything organized. I want to apply for scholarships and get a job.

I don't know why I only kept resentment in my heart for my mother. This person has given me everything I know and own.

Every Sunday I go to church. I ask God for forgiveness. When I get home, I do something that ruins the entire day. It could be cursing, lying, or disrespecting my brother either by screaming and cursing at him.

I want to be a real Christian so bad but I always fail at it. I must be doing something wrong. I noticed how when scientists are working on a project that fails, they try again and again and again with different methods until they get it right. But not me. I noticed all I do is go to church, pray to God to forgive me, and then do the same next time.

Punishments

1.

Me: You're going to hell for cursing.
Brother: No I'm not, cause I'm a baby.
Me: But you know right from wrong, and you know that's wrong.

2.

Brother: I hate you
Me: Then you're going to hell.
Brother: No I'm not.
Me: I hate you.
Brother: I don't care.

He points his middle finger at me, and I say, "God is watching."

Brother: No he's not. I can't even see him.

Brother: Fuck you.
Me: Hell is a scary place.
Brother: How do you know?

Janice Meredith at her salon, by Susan Henry.

Saved Up for Me

In the hallway of John Mac, Ms. Richardson keeps up a bulletin board with her successful students. She calls it her Cosmetology Hall of Fame. She puts pictures of students who graduated years ago with how much they make doing hair and where their shops are located. Sometimes she connects her current students with them.

One day she told me she had been telling one of her old students, Janice, about me. She said, "This is a really good opportunity for you, Susan." I was so excited, but at the same time, I felt unprepared because I wasn't registered to get my license. I kept putting it off until she asked again and then made me call her on my cell phone. She asked me, "When can you come?" I went to see her on a Tuesday when she works in her office. She asked me, "How serious are you about this because I've had young girls come in and run off with their boyfriends since we get off late sometimes."

I told her, "I don't even have a boyfriend."

She said, "You look like you're a quiet girl," and gave me a rundown on how the shop runs.

She asked me if I drove, and I said no. She lived down the street from me, and said she could pick me up. She knows my mom's not around and she tells me if I need anyone to talk to, I can come to her.

At first, I was as tired as I've ever been. I'd come home with my plan in my head already, "Okay, in 30 minutes I'll be in bed." But being in the shop was good therapy for me. I always laugh when I'm at work. Women there talk about interesting, funny things. Once I heard the tail end of a conversation where a woman was explaining to her hairdresser, "...my boyfriend's girlfriend, that's why I'm burnt up!" I just listen most of the time. Sometimes I think God had this job saved up for me. Maybe the struggles I've gone through make me appreciate it more.

Simply Divine Full Service Salon, by Susan Henry.

Both pages: Hair and nails, by Susan Henry.

Susan's designs, courtesy of Susan Henry.

Design

At school, I liked to visit my counselor, Mrs. Bethquit, in her office. I was concerned about what I was going to do after graduation if my papers didn't get in order. I helped her with paperwork and one time even told her a story about Johnboy.

At home, I was designing and making a few dresses. My brother took pictures and then I put them in my school binder. When Ms. Bethquit saw my designs and photographs she said, "You should sign up with FINO, the Fashion Institute of New Orleans." It was too late for me that year, but she gave me tickets for their fashion show during the summer. Her daughter, Tiffany, was in charge of everything. At the show

the photographer asked me and a friend to help him take some test shots, and gave me his card, saying, "Email me so I can send you your pictures." I printed them out and made frames to put in my room.

My 11th grade year, I signed up for FINO. It all started with field trips. Every other Thursday we left school and went to work at a building in the East that consisted of many small offices. The workshops included photography, sewing and design, makeup, and modeling. I worked in the sewing and designing. Some Thursdays we worked at our offices and sometimes we all got together in the main room to listen to visitors talk about their work.

Not only did I have a space to work at with FINO, but my uncle Henry and my dad rented a new house just around the corner from my grams. I loved it. My brother and I both had our own rooms, and mine was the biggest. I turned it into a studio with my sewing machine and computer. I painted the frames of the windows white to make it look fresh and hung up my pictures on the wall.

Before the ending of the year, we had to turn in a final project made up of pictures and a short essay about the student working on it. Photographers had to take pictures of people to put in the portfolio, makeup artists had to show their work through pictures, models had to have pictures taken of them, and designers had to have pictures of their work as well as turning in something they worked on. People who didn't turn in projects couldn't participate in mini-camp during the summer, but they could still be in the fashion show.

I wrote my essay that day. I told the story of growing up in La Ceiba and how my interest in fashion and hair started with my mom. As I started writing, I felt better about our relationship. I went to Walmart with my dad to buy a printer, construction paper, clear folders, and sheet protectors to make it look good.

I was finished a week early. Two female students who were working on their modeling projects had given up. They said they had no way to print out their pictures, they didn't know what to write about or what to do. I talked to them separately, invited them to my house and one slept over. My room was a working studio that night. I didn't go to sleep until three in the morning, working on their hair and makeup, and then taking pictures. One wore a leather jacket I made. I provided them with the folders and the paper,

Susan's new house, by Susan Henry.

and printed out the pictures. I felt like I had everything I needed, for this project and life in general.

During the mini-camp, we went to a fabric store in the suburbs called Hancock. I was used to going to Walmart where the selection is limited. The fabric is geared more towards house decorating instead fashion. When I walked into Hancock, there was fabric everywhere, from black to purple and red. All the fabrics were arranged by color and texture. I walked around looking in every corner, and then came back to the front and started again, this time feeling the different fabrics—I was going for material that I knew I could work with. I could picture what I could do with it as I felt it. For some reason, I was fixated on pockets, and ended up making high waist shorts and a silver dress with pockets.

FINO logo designed by Susan, courtesy of the Fashion Institute of New Orleans.

We all worked hard for few weeks in preparation for the fashion show. Some worked on one outfit they wore for the show while others like Gloria and me worked on several outfits. Gloria was a former student at FINO and was now working for them. She came up to me one afternoon and introduced herself and asked, "You're Susan, right? I'm Johnboy's best friend. I know all about you."

I was at a loss for words. I didn't know what my relationship with Johnboy was. Gloria and I got to be cool.

Days before the show, I went on Channel Four to speak about the fashion show on June 18. I was nervous but managed to not show it until that day. We practiced asking questions to each other that we though they might ask. Tansy, one of the FINO workers, asked the questions.

Tansy: What are you wearing?

Susan: I'm wearing a black cocktail dress that I designed myself.

Tansy: It's made of brocade material.

Susan: I won't remember all of that.

The questions went on. I went home saying, "brocade" and went to the office the next day saying "crocade." I was sure I was saying the right name.

Susan: It's crocade, right?

Blane: No, it's brocade, silly!

Susan: Oh my God, I'm going to forget. By the time we are on T.V. I'm going to mess up.

I kept saying it over and over, and they laughed at me.

It was time. We were on the air and Blane talked about the Institute. When Sally-Ann Roberts asked me to stand and speak about my design, I never looked at the camera.

Sally-Ann: Is this one of your designs?

Susan: Yes, ma'am. This is a cocktail dress made of cro-brocade material that I made myself.

I was sure Blane and Tansy would be shaking their head.

Sally-Ann: Did you use a pattern?

Susan: Yes, I did.

After we left the station, we headed to get some breakfast at one of Blane's favorite places. As we walked in, a lady pointed me out, "You made the hell out of that dress!" They talked about us as if we were local celebrities and it felt nice.

We also did an interview on Q93, the hip hop and R&B radio station in town. Wild Wayne was going to be one of the emcee of the fashion show. He talked about hosting and then asked us to introduce ourselves and wanted to know if we had any special shout-outs. Craig, who is very attached to his girlfriend, gave a shout out to her. That was sweet. It was my turn.

Susan: Nope. I have no one to shout out for.

Wild Wayne: No boyfriend? No friends, no one?

Susan: Nope.

Makeup before the show, courtesy of the Fashion Institute of New Orleans.

It was Sam's turn, who was always crushing on me.

Sam: Well, I would like to give a shout-out to Susan.

Everyone in the room laughed. His best friend Edward pointed out that he didn't even get a shout out.

The day before the show I worked on my hair, my nails, and my lashes in front of the full length mirrors in my room. I was so excited. We went to Generation Hall that morning to practice on the runway and set up for the show.

I thought I was going to have a big showing when Kenneth, my friend from church, came by before the show to show his support. But he got held up at work and couldn't make it that night. Janice, my boss from the salon, called to wish me good luck because the shop was too busy for her to come. At the last minute, my brother mentioned that he and my dad wanted to come, but I knew my dad was just joking. It was time for the show to begin and I was the first one up. I wasn't nervous at all. I was ready.

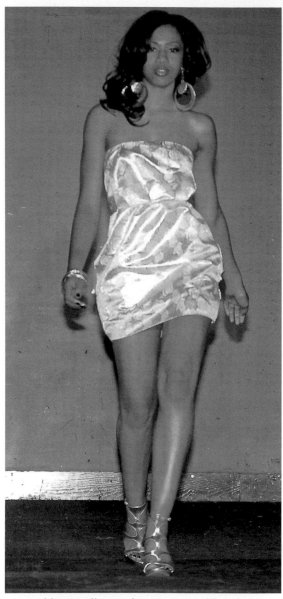

Susan modeling one of her own designs, courtesy of the Fashion Institute of New Orleans.

As I walked down the runway I kept my head straight forward. When I got to the end, I stopped and posed. I heard my name being called. I knew my friend Domonique bought a ticket, and I was happy to see her there, but the person who was the most excited was Mrs. Richardson. She kept calling my name and asking me to turn toward her so that she could get a picture.

The end of the show was just as exciting as the beginning. Bobby Valentino closed the show with his performance.

When it was time for me to leave, a news reporter came up to me and asked me some questions. John-boy approached me as the interview took place, but I couldn't even turn to him.

One of Susan's dresses being modeled on the runway, courtesy of the Fashion Institute of New Orleans.

Above: Gloria on the runway. *Right:* Susan on the runway. Photographs courtesy of the Fashion Institute of New Orleans.

Susan styling her hair before the fashion show, courtesy of the Fashion Institute of New Orleans.

Black Hair

In the fashion show, I felt glamorous with my long curly hair extensions. I began by braiding my hair into a pattern that went with a style I was looking for. Once I had the pattern, I sewed the hair extensions on the braids, making sure was balanced and even. I didn't want too much hair around my face or not enough.

When I growing up in La Ceiba, I'd do my own hair—giving myself relaxers and putting my hair up in ponytails. When I saw black women on T.V., I thought that I would have straight, long hair in a matter of months of arriving in the States. I didn't realize that they were mostly weaves.

By the time we actually left, my mom had to cut my hair because it was extremely damaged from a relaxer that had been left in too long. I knew I wasn't supposed to wet it everyday, but I couldn't resist sneaking off to the lake to go swimming. My mom cut into a short bob and I grew it out again to my shoulders in New Orleans.

I first encountered weaves at drug store. I wanted to try it, so I bought the glue and the hair and my mom put it in. We were experimenting because it was her first time, too. After wearing them a couple of times, I started noticing that my hair was breaking off because of the glue. I didn't want to use it any-more but I was used to the longer, fuller look.

My uncle Henry brought me to his girlfriend's house and she sewed in a weave. I could keep the extensions in for weeks she did such a good job. With this new and improved method, my hair grew back. When I'm with one of my clients, I refuse to use glue on them so they can have healthy hair.

My boss, Janice, tells me I need to know how to work with short hair because short can be beauti-ful as well. When I look at her, she's beautiful. She's been teaching me how to do the spikes and work with colors. Just recently someone told me, "Makeup is pretty, a weave is pretty. But when you can wake up next to a woman without makeup and with her own hair, and she still is beautiful to you, that's real beauty." I thought about that a lot and to prove it to myself, I took out my weave and put my hair in two plaits. I felt just as cute.

Susan with her natural hair in braids, by Rachel Breunlin.

Above: Carolina Gallop, by Abram Himelstein. *Right:* Program for Carolina Gallop's fashion show that Susan attended at the Blue Nile.

Interview with Fashion Designer, Carolina Gallop

As I was finishing up my book, I learned about a fashion show in New Orleans run by a woman from La Ceiba. Everyone at the Neighborhood Story Project wanted me to go, but I was reluctant. I didn't think it was going to be as fashion forward as it was. But the show was cool. I loved all of her designs, and asked her if she wouldn't mind being interviewed. She said, "Oh, that's wonderful! You're from La Ceiba? I'd love to." It felt good that someone knew my place and was interested in the same things as I was.

The interview was awesome. I had so many questions for her. I related the stories about school and family to mine. She explained the ways that she feels connected to both New Orleans and La Ceiba. I feel like that, too.

Susan: Where are you from?

Carolina: I grew up in a place called La Ceiba, Honduras, which is so much like New Orleans in that it's 24 hours a day—music, entertainment, food. People come from all over Central America to go to La Ceiba—just like people come from all over the U.S. to come to New Orleans. We have all the best live music, which includes a lot of ranchera, bachata, reggaetón.

S: Did you grow up speaking English or have any connection with the West Indies?

C: My grandfather was Jamaican and my father was half Indian and half Jamaican. I grew up speaking English and Spanish—mostly a lot of Spanish. In the house, my dad wanted us to speak English because he didn't want us to get stuck always speaking Spanish and not knowing both languages.

When I was a kid, my sisters, brothers and I went to a private Catholic school and a lot of our teachers were British nuns. We had a lot of that British English. I didn't realize until I grew up how lucky we were. A lot of kids in Central America are so poor, they can't go to school because they can't afford to buy the uniform.

S: I don't know much about the history of La Ceiba. How is it different than other parts of Honduras?

C: We were a shipping port like New Orleans—there used to be a lot of shipping activities that went on between La Ceiba and New Orleans and that's why you have a big population of Hondurans living here in New Orleans. They all came through with these shipping companies in La Ceiba. You have all these people that get off the ship and want to drink and

Carolina's grandmother in Roatán, courtesy of Carolina Gallop.

party 24 hours because they've been on a ship for five days straight. That's how we got to be a party town. If you go further inland, you have mountains, lakes, and rivers. But where we live, and why a lot of people come from all over Central America—including Cuba—to La Ceiba is because we have all the entertainment and we have the ocean right there.

S: Can you tell us about your family?

C: I come from a family of eight. I've got four sisters and four brothers. My dad passed away years ago. My mother still lives in Boston. I have two sisters and a brother in Honduras and I've got one sister and two brothers in Boston. One brother, unfortunately, passed away when he was only 25 years old.

My grandma is 94 years old, and still lives in Boston. The family she worked for in Roatán left when some kind of war was about to get started in Honduras. They were a young, Jewish couple and decided to go back to Boston. They told my grandmother they were going to send for her one day. A couple of years later, she got that visa in the mail. She came to the United States, and lived in Brookline, Massachusetts—one of the most prominent areas in Boston—and worked for them. They helped her out with everything, including learning how to look for and buy a house. My grandma bought a house over 50 years ago and she's still living in that same big, beautiful house in Boston.

She brought us all up to the States. We were very vulnerable when we came to this country. We were young. We had been sheltered all our lives. One of my big challenges was with my sister—she came to America and got deported because she was really heavy on drugs. I told her I couldn't help her until she changed her ways. Miraculously, she's clean. She's been off drugs for almost ten years—and I'm talkin about crack here. She's my sister again—she's fat, she owns her own house, she has a son, she's a preacher. I'm writing a book around her life, which is going to take a long time because we're going back from childhood to her fall and her rise.

S: What did your parents do for a living?

C: My mom was a homemaker. When I was about two years old, she left and came to America and my father raised us. My dad was an architect. I remember going back to Honduras after leaving when I was 13. I went into a bank and gave the banker my last name. He goes, "Are you related to Señor Gallop?" and I said, "Yeah, that's my dad." He goes, "Come here, I want to show you something." He walks me

Top: Carolina and her siblings in La Ceiba. *Bottom:* Carolina's father, William Gallop. Photographs courtesy of Carolina Gallop.

outside the bank and there's a gold plaque outside the building: the architect was William Gallop, Sr. who was my grandfather. I was floored like, "Oh my God, that's where my design talent came from." I didn't know he had built so much.

S: What was your childhood like?

C: Awesome. All I did was climb trees and swim in the ocean. The beach was right across the street from where we lived. We had a huge fence around our big property and we were not allowed to go to the ocean unless we were with an adult. I was running behind my brothers, a little tomboy: "No, I'm not gonna comb my hair and sit like a lady. I'm hanging out with the guys." We used to have rabbits running through our properties —parakeets and iguanas everywhere.

I was heartbroken when my dad put us on a plane to come to the States. I'd never been away from my dad. I cried the whole time on the plane. I remember the Pan Am flight attendant told my sister, "Here, give her this," and she gave me a nip of alcohol to shut me up.

As a teenager, I went, "All right, my dad's not here anymore. I'm gonna act up." There were no trees to climb, no oceans to go into. During the blizzard of 1978, I saw all that snow and I couldn't believe it. We played in it without shoes and jackets and people were looking at us like we were crazy. We're like, "We're from Honduras. We don't know."

I'm went to an American school where my English is Honduran English. It's not that it's broken—I spoke better English than most of the kids—it's just that I had my own dialect. I remember the teacher said,

Carolina at the beach in La Ceiba, courtesy of Carolina Gallop.

"Sit down," and I said, "Yes, sir." And he said, "Don't get smart with me either." It was so bad, I couldn't pay attention to what the teacher said because all the students are acting up.

S: I'm going through the same thing.

C: Oh, you are?

S: Yeah, it's the same exact thing you're saying.

C: We're a Third World country but our education—like Cuba—is unbelievable.

S: Did you ever visit the bay islands?

C: Oh my God, I love Roatán. As a matter of fact, I was about to book my flight and then they kicked Zelaya out, and I said, "Not a good time for me to go to Honduras." But I spent a whole week in Roatán last year. I went snorkeling. One of my girlfriends went scuba diving. They have a big shrimp festival every year.

Roatán has changed a lot. It's still very beautiful but there aren't that many trees because they've made way for buildings. Just like the French Quarter in New Orleans, the property values have gone up so much. My grandfather had a lot of land in Roatán way before what's his name, from Microsoft, went over there and bought a huge piece of property. Europeans are buying up a lot—they have a flight that goes every day from Italy to Roatán. It's dollars and *lempira*.

A lot of my family never went back after coming here and I'm like, "Y'all don't know what you missing out." I have a piece of property where I'm about to build a house on the beach. I don't plan on moving permanently to Honduras but I'd like to be able to stay in my own house when I go.

S: Why did you move to New Orleans?

C: By accident, sort of. I was living in Venice Beach in Los Angeles and there was a big earthquake that rocked my world. At four in the morning, I woke up and felt the ground ripple. It freaked me out. I said, "Oh, I've gotta get out of here. Where am I gonna go?"

A few months later, my cousin came to New Orleans to open up the House of Blues. She calls and says, "Come to New Orleans, it's scary down here. I don't know anybody here." And I said, "When I was a little girl in Honduras, adults always talked about California and *Nueva Orleans*." I said, "Yes, I've always wanted to go see New Orleans."

I get off the plane and I'm like, "Oh shoot, this looks like Honduras. I can't live here. This is like a Third World." I had that thing where I grew up in Boston, this big beautiful city, and then in LA, where it's on the beach.

The French Quarter felt so closed in. I went uptown to St. Charles and all saw those houses and thought, "I could live up here for sure." Then I started driving around the back neighborhoods and was like, "Ooh, my God—no, get me out of here." But I went back to LA and realized I missed New Orleans. How can I miss a place I don't even know?

I came back again and really looked at it with open eyes and an open heart and I said, "This is where I'm gonna live one day. I think I'm gonna die and grow old in this city." It was almost like they were in La Ceiba because the people are sweet. They have the same personality. It's not like I didn't walk around seeing a lot of the youth gangster attitude, but it was also really humbling to be around young people that were playing music and doing art.

S: What do you think of your life in New Orleans as a Honduran woman from La Ceiba?

C: Busy. You hear that phone? That phone will ring 20 times all day. When people meet me they'll go, "Where are you from? You're not from New Orleans." I'm like, "Well, I'm from New Orleans but I was born and raised in Honduras." There's this stand back thing, like, "Oh cool, wow, I've always wanted to go to Honduras," or, "What's Honduras like?" which is what let me come up with the idea to do an excursion to Honduras. People are waiting for me to do that.

S: Sometimes people tell me I'm not really black because I'm from another country. Has that ever happened to you?

C: In Boston, a lot of the Irish are very racist, but the Irish are racist against the Italians and the Polish.

It was almost not even about the skin. Where I lived in Dorchester, it was a very Irish and Jewish neighborhood. My grandma and another family were two of the first black families in that neighborhood that bought houses, and then a lot of blacks and Hispanics started moving into the neighborhood, and a lot of people started going out of the city into the suburbs. Today, all the Latinos and blacks are being moved out into the suburbs and the whites are coming back into the city because that's where it's at. The younger generations are saying, "Fuck you mom, I'm going back to the city."

Before I got there, they had just started doing busing. That first year in school, "Roots" came out. It was a big miniseries and the teacher said for everybody to watch it. I hate to say it, but it's true—I didn't know anything about slavery because they never taught us slavery in school in Honduras. They weren't teaching us slavery in high school in Boston either. Nobody really talked about it. They always talked about John Adams.

When the movie came out, a lot of black people were angry. Like, "Wow, damn, we didn't know all this shit." They were picking on all the white kids and all the white kids were scared because they're like, "We got nothing to do with that." I had a friend named Rosemary Cushing—an Irish girl. We were in class and these little black girls were trying to mess with her, and somebody pulled her hair. I'm like, "Hey, don't do that," in my accent. They're like, "Mind your business." I said, "No, pull my hair like that. Why you picking on somebody else? We just want to learn. Why don't you stop acting up so we can all learn something?"

Everyday Rosemary and I went to her house. Her sister used to have peanut butter and jelly sandwiches ready for us so we could do our homework. I remember one time, we were driving with her family, and her uncle was like, "Yeah, these fucking niggers." Rosemary slaps him upside the head, "Uncle Bobby, don't say that!" He goes, "Oh, I'm not worried about Carolina. She's not black." I said, "Well, yes I am. That's my color. I'm from Honduras but I'm still—" He goes, "I'm not a racist. It's just some people." I was at their house everyday eating and hanging out, but she never had a black friend.

So yeah, I got that a lot growing up, "You're from Honduras, you're not black." I'm like, "There's a lot of Garifunas from Honduras. You look at them and they're black." Maybe it's because I speak another language. You know how you fill out those forms and they like say "white, black, Hispanic"? You can say "black but not Hispanic" or "Hispanic—not black". I don't know what to answer. I check "black" and "Hispanic." That confuses them. If I had Irish in me, I'd go "white" and they'd be like, "Wait a minute. This girl's messing with us." But why should I leave any of them out?

I don't really label myself. I don't say I grew up Latina in Honduras. Sure, I speak Spanish. I'm dark-skinned. I'm lighter than most, but I'm still, if I don't open my mouth, you don't know. My accent is from everywhere and nowhere at all.

S: Where do you live in New Orleans?

C: I lived in the Quarter for seven years and then I bought a house in Gentilly that got water. My husband and I sold it. After the storm, we got really lucky because we had a friend who lent us his condo in Destin, Florida for a whole year on the beach. It was great, but I was in New Orleans every week. It was just super weird because here was all this sadness going on in New Orleans and then all the beauty on the beach in Destin. They didn't get hit by any of the hurricanes that year. I felt a little guilty living in such a beautiful condo.

Once I moved back to New Orleans, I wanted to be part of the rebuilding. We lost a lot of our medical crew here. A lot of people who evacuated don't realize that. New Orleans is broken. We don't have enough hospitals. I went online and found a grant to become a paramedic.

This year, I went from January to August in school, studying as a basic paramedic. I had September to make the clothes and promote my fashion show. It worked out pretty good, but I worked my butt off to do it. A lot of people wanted to buy pieces that night, but I didn't want to sell them. I've been asked to do this fashion show in the French Market so I'm gonna take some of those pieces and throw them back on the runway. Do your fashion but you've always got to have something else because there's no instant money there.

S: How did you get started in fashion?

C: I always wanted to be a doctor. It's been a dream of mine since I was a kid and saw those Red Cross nurses in Honduras. But fashion, it happened accidentally. When I first moved to New Orleans, I had plenty of time on my hands. I started sewing and making clothes. My cousin came over and she goes, "What are all those clothes?" I said, "I made them." She goes, "What?! Let's do a fashion show."

I asked the Fashion Café if I could use their space. I went to Kinko's and printed some flyers, put them out all over the place, and my first show packed out the house. That's when the label was given to me: "Fashion designer." I didn't look at myself as a fashion designer. The people in the city were the ones that elevated me to that fashion design. New Orleans made me who I am. It's gonna make me a doctor eventually.

S: Do you have any fashion heroes?

C: One of my favorite fashion heroes passed away last year and that was Yves Saint Laurent. I love the big hats, the big bows and the juicy silks and the little tight long dresses, the tuxedo jackets. My fashion show last year was a tribute to Yves Saint Laurent. So I had a lot of tuxedo-type pieces that I dedicated to his memory. This year, as you all know, Michael Jackson passed away and I did a tribute to Michael Jackson for his influence on me in fashion, but also dancing, music, and all that.

Jean-Paul Gaultier, Vivienne Westwood—designers that go all out. I used to make the ball gowns and big fluffy things because I was going to a lot of balls and wanted high end clients. Then I realized I wanted to make affordable dresses for women and young girls. I don't want to make 1,500 dollar dresses, 500 dollar dresses all the time because that takes away from the fun of being a designer for me. Harold Clarke is a great designer. He makes those types of dresses and everybody says, "Oh my gosh, you should make dresses like Harold Clarke," and I'm like, "I could, but I choose not to. I make the little dresses and some pants and throw it on the runway." I am working on trying to start a boutique—a designer's show house for different designers. Don't know how I'm gonna have the time after January because I start school again.

S: What do you think of the fashion industry?

C: I like designers like Vivienne Westwood and Jean-Paul Gaultier and Balenciaga. They're cutting edge fashion. They make things that other designers copy. They have a great time as opposed to let's hurry up and put it out.

For a lot of people, it's about making a lot of money as opposed to loving it as an art. I'm an artist and I make clothes. It's easy to have a fashion line when you can go and hire somebody to draft your pattern, tell them what you want, they design it and make the pattern for you, send your stuff to China to have it made or to some dressmaker in LA and have it made. To me, that takes the fun away. I want to make all my pieces. Then I can have the favorite ones duplicated. A fashion designer is not just designing. It's actually trying to make your own pattern and sewing your own original piece.

S: How do the men in your life treat your work?

C: My dad's dead, but I'm sure he would be very pleased that I decided to pick up a ruler because that seems to be in the bloodline. Growing up, my dad had, on the walls, all these sketches. We were not allowed to go into this room and I'd peek in there and pick up a ruler. If you're a kid and you walk into my studio, it's kind of like that.

A lot of the things I do, I taught myself. Pick up a pattern, you read it, you copy what they're telling you to do, but you add your own design as well— your own ideas. My husband has always been very supportive. If it wasn't for him, I probably wouldn't ever have time to sit down and design because he was paying all the bills and working. I was the one sitting in the house making clothes. I started making my clothes out of boredom and then realized it was a way to make money as well. We've been married for 13 years and he's still supporting me but I'm still not sitting on my leg going, "Oh well," and watching T.V. I'm getting out there in the community. I want to give back.

S: Have any children?

C: No. No time for kids, baby.

S: Do you have any advice for me if I want a career in fashion? Well, I do.

C: If you want a career in fashion, all I have to say is keep doing it. Don't let anybody discourage you because a lot of times it's overwhelming. As a fashion designer, if you start making pieces where you're trying to sell a dress for 200 dollar then you're gonna have a hard time. If you don't spend a lot of money on the fabric and you sew dresses for 50-75 dollars and make ten or 12 of those dresses, you can make a little bit of money every week. You go and set up your own little sale and do a fashion show a week or two after that.

S: Like for me, it's the same as you. I was bored and started making clothes for Barbie dolls. And then I got my first sewing machine when I was like 13 and started cutting up my clothes that I had that were too big for me.

C: Recycling.

S: Yes!

C: You didn't even know it.

Susan's grandparent's house next to the house she had to leave, by Susan Henry.

Interview with Felipe Smith, Part II

My dad moved us back over to my grandparents' house. Once again, I thought it was just temporary, but we never moved back. I still went over there by myself, but I knew it wasn't going to be ours much longer. I didn't want to let my room go. One day, when I was at work, my grams called and said, "They've thrown all of your stuff out."

I didn't know how to feel. Deep down, I knew none of it was mine. I started to feel like the only things that belong to me are my talent and my stories. For a long time, I didn't want to tell the stories. I felt like, "Who cares?" I didn't think it was important. But, just as my mom and other women passed their talents on to me, I want to pass my sto- *ries on to inspire others. I've loved learning about hair and fashion. I feel that if women like my mother, Mrs. Rich, and Janice took their time to teach me so much, I can just as well bless someone else. What's mine will still be mine. It will be up to them to make it their own. As I was getting ready to finish writing, I thought I'd ask Felipe what the impact of books are around the world, and why one like mine might be special here in New Orleans.*

Felipe Smith, by Lindsey Darnell.

Susan: Why are books important to the world?

Felipe: Do you know the expression, "double consciousness"? This is an expression that W.E.B. Du Bois used in *The Souls of Black Folk*, which you're going to have to read when you get further in your studies. He was saying is that all black people in America have two ways of seeing themselves. They see themselves as the people that they are in their houses, in their churches, in their communities. They know themselves through just basic living experiences. But the second way that they know themselves is through they way they are represented in magazines, newspapers, the television reports. The people they see on television wading through the water with flat screen T.V.s on their back coming out of Walmart are not the people that they know from living in the neighborhood. It's two completely different versions of

their reality. W.E.B. Du Bois was talking about this as a kind of split mentality that doesn't allow a black person to really get a real sense of identity. "Am I the person I think I am or am I the person they think I am?" You have to be aware of both and you have to have a strategy of dealing with both.

Well, you have a variation of that because even within your sort of normal routine you have two consciousnesses. You have the consciousness of a person who is an outsider within this community and then you're in this community which is thought of as being outside of American experience itself. It's a very complicated set of experiences.

DuBois said, "Okay, if this is the condition that we experience on a day-to-day basis, then why don't we make that the way we tell the story?" In other words, it goes from being a kind of split personality problem to actually being a way of telling the story. It's like when people would marginalize, exclude, or put you into a different category when they find out that you didn't grow up in this neighborhood or that neighborhood. They automatically reclassify you. They heard "Honduran" and they immediately thought, "Spanish-speaking person who knows no English." That was their image of you. The question that arises is, "How did that make you feel?" Use that feeling as a way of coming to grips with the person that you want to project in the story.

Books are important because New Orleans is not the world and in order to figure out what the meaning of your experience is you have to be able to put it into a context of people who have other realities, other experiences, other frames of reference.

New Orleans is a place that could continue forever as an oral-based society because you have one generation telling another generation all of this important cultural data that could be passed along. A lot of it is performed in the streets. So it's participant/observer kind of information and you could live a very normative New Orleans lifestyle without having any books to explain anything else to you.

Most people never get put into a context where you get people to synthesize their experience for you into a form where you can understand their life just in a short period of time. Most people you know through common experiences. You get to know them gradually over a long period of time, whereby you have interactions and then more information becomes available. A book significantly shortens the time span in which you can process that information about other people's experiences. It allows you to lengthen your productive life by not having to have interactions with a multitude of people to gain access to their information and their experiences. You can take a shortcut. You can read x number of books and get that kind of information and what that allows you to do then is to play the game at a higher level.

You can then interact with other people living in other places based on having a shared experience of reading the same books and the book then becomes the place at which you meet other people and then begin to incorporate their experiences into your knowledge base. It's a way of connecting with history. And for your generation, just imagine how much more is opened up to you. Books allow you to explore dimensions of yourself that may not be called forward by your immediate context—things that you don't realize that you might have an affinity to because it's not part of your immediate experience. You can find out through books that, "Wow, I really like this concept or this group of people's culture. I want to go there." It may be an impulse that you would never have had if you just remained within your own little sphere.

So the world is really beginning to be divided among people who have access to outside information and people who don't and for many, many people that's the single difference in terms of the direction their lives go. You have a lot of people who end up living their parents' lives with a few more consumer products thrown in, fewer children. But in order to move to a sort of another level of possibility, you need to be able to access other people's experiences and not be locked into the experiences of people who are part of your immediate world and that's where books come in.

I mean, that's why I think this project is valuable. Inevitably, somebody is going to come across your story and even if their background is not the same, it's going to help them to understand themselves better simply by seeing how you had to adapt in order to be able to become a high functioning person in society—the way that you were able make your cultural heritage an advantage for you in your life- -something that could be an enhancement to who you are as opposed to something that you're trying to escape from.

NSP AFTERWORD

December 2009

It has been a long four years for the Neighborhood Story Project since the last series of books by John McDonogh students came out. In June of 2005, we were riding high, with five books by high school students circulating the city and neighborhoods were they were written. After Harry Potter, they were the best sellers in the city.

And in August of 2005 we were back at John McDonogh, with 60 applicants for the next round of book-making, and went home for a weekend of sorting applications. On Monday, the levees failed, and the applications were waiting on Rachel's kitchen table when we got back to town seven weeks later, a grim reminder of one more thing lost.

The NSP set about the work it knew, making books with Nine Times Social and Pleasure Club, making posters about the Seventh Ward, and a book of community gathering spots- Cornerstones. But through it all we wanted to go back to John McDonogh and hear what was happening in teenage-land.

So in the fall of 2007, we went recruiting at John Mac. We were holding the first round of books, relics of the pre-storm era, and very few of the new students had heard of them. There were five brave souls who signed up for a class in book-making. Daron Crawford, Susan Henry, Kareem Kennedy, Kenneth Phillips, and Pernell Russell.

The first part was the easiest. We read the first round of NSP books and the classics like: *Life and Death on the South Side of Chicago*, and Sherman Alexie's *Lone Ranger and Tonto First Fight in Heaven*.

And then we started on the two and a half year journey of writing our stories. We wrote about life before Katrina, and some of the Katrina experience, but we mostly worked on Documenting the Now.

The Now was ever-changing: Daron moved from house to house, and studio to studio. Kareem went from high school student to Delgado student. Pernell went from nearly care-free (dancing, making clothes) to dealing with loss. Susan's career in fashion and cosmetology went from theoretical to real. Kenneth worked on his anger management, while getting learning about his past.

We began to talk about the need to have something at stake in the book- the need to represent our struggles and not just the things that we wanted people to know about our lives. Or as Kareem Kennedy put it to everyone, "People want to read your mind to ease their mind."

And so we started in on the writing the hard parts. We went to where the projects were in the process of being torn down. Sneaking in through holes in fences, we roamed where the thousands lived, now desolate and post-apocalyptic. We went to the new spaces, shotgun doubles, ranch homes in the suburbs, and we wrote to make sense of the changes.

Rachel taught interviewing and ethnography- how to de-familiarize yourself with your surroundings and connect your personal stories to the larger cultures of New Orleans. Abram taught writing styles. Lea and Lindsey went with the writers to interview and photograph.

During 2008 we kept at it, interviewing family, former neighbors, other people who could help broaden their perspectives on themes in the books.

In March of 2008 the NSP published *The House of Dance and Feathers: A Museum by Ronald Lewis*, and the writers got to see their first NSP book release party- in Ronald's backyard in the Lower Ninth Ward, Mardi Gras Indians and Brass Bands. Two hundred people dancing in the rain.

As Rachel turned her attention from editing *The House of Dance and Feathers*, toward working on building up the structures of the four books the work kicked into overdrive. Weekends became an abstract idea, as writers and NSP staff started to live in our office in Seventh Ward. We took occasional breaks to go back out and get more photos, or to get the interviewees more involved in the editing process.

In September of 2009 we printed out what we had and gave copies to family and friends and impartial readers. They came together as book committees, telling us what they liked and what the books needed to feel finished. We took notes, gave ourselves a weekend off, and then got back on the horse.

October was the end of the road. We had to weigh what pieces stayed in, how to tell the untold parts. Hard decisions as the idea of books met the reality of paper and print. Late nights and early mornings led to this- four new books, five new authors, and a return to the roots of the NSP.

NSP'S HUGE LIST OF THANK-YOUS

Our first and biggest thank-you to our authors and their families: Daron Crawford, Susan Henry, Kareem Kennedy, Kenneth Phillips, and Pernell Russell. It has been two great years of getting to know y'all, and a huge honor to be so involved in your lives. We are proud of your work, and feel blessed to have become family. We look forward to knowing y'all and reading y'all for years to come.

To the mighty University of New Orleans—the College of Liberal Arts, the College of Education, and UNO Press: We are grateful and proud to be a part of the University community. Thank you to Chancellor Ryan, Susan Krantz, Rick Barton, Bob Cashner, Joe King, and Anthony Cipolone. In Anthropology, thank you to David Beriss, Jeffrey Ehrenreich, and Martha Ward. In the College of Education, thank you to Jim Meza, Andre Perry, and April Whatley Bedford. At UNO Press, Bill Lavender and GK Darby.

To all the people who have supported the NSP, thank you. Huge gratitude to all of the writers at the write-a-thon, without whom we could not have made this milestone. We look forward to out-writing last year's amazingness.

To the Lupin Foundation. Thank you for your consistent support over the years. These books could not have happened without you.

To our John McDonogh Senior High/ RSD family—Principal Gerald Debose, Antoinette Pratcher, Dawn Greay, Alicia Carter Watts, Shawon Bernard, Brother Jamal Robertson, Deborah Richardson, Nira Cooper and all of the other teachers at the Mac. Thank you for working with us and for being so supportive of the efforts of the NSP.

Thank you to the Cowan Family and Jewish Funds for Justice. Your gift kept us going, and Paul's legacy continues to inspire us.

To Gareth, thank you for going above and beyond, once again, to balance a crazy amount of work with beautiful design.

For getting us ready to go to press, Felicia McCarren, Jordan Flaherty, Siobhan Flahive McKieran, Ariella Cohen, GK Darby, Bill Lavender, Hot Iron Press, and Eve Abrams.

To the Bard Early College in New Orleans program and Stephen Tremaine: thank you for being an awesome partner in this work.

To our board—Petrice Sams Abiodun, Susan Krantz. Corlita Mahr Spreen, Troy Materre, Helen Regis, and Emelda Wylie. It has been a great journey with y'all, and we are looking forward to more.

Thank you to the Zeitoun Foundation for supporting the work. Your unsolicited gift was a huge boost to our organization, and your story of reclaiming against great odds has been part of our inspiration.

And to our families: Dan and Max Omar Etheridge; Cynthia Breunlin, Doug Breunlin and Nanci Gordon, Megan Etheridge, and Kate, Tommaso, and Zoe Weichmann (for stepping in to help take care of Rachel's men while she was on editing lockdown); Nolan Marshall, Tessa Corthell, Shana Sassoon, Phyllis, Linda and Jerry, the Hsiangs, the Downings, the Darnells: thank you for being our family through this process. We could not have done it without you, and we are glad we didn't have to try.

Viva New Orleans

Rachel Breunlin, Lindsey Darnell, Lea Downing and Abram Himelstein

Neighborhood Story Project